Impertinent Decorum

The Cassell Lesbian and Gay Studies list offers a broad-based platform to lesbian, gay and bisexual writers for the discussion of contemporary issues and for the promotion of new ideas and research.

COMMISSIONING:
Steve Cook
Roz Hopkins

CONSULTANTS:
Liz Gibbs
Christina Ruse
Peter Tatchell

Impertinent Decorum

Gay Theatrical Manoeuvres

Ian Lucas

CASSELL

Cassell
Villiers House
41/47 Strand
London WC2N 5JE

387 Park Avenue South
New York, NY 10016-8810

First published 1994

British Library Cataloguing-in-Publication Data
A catalogue record for this book is available from the British Library.

Library of Congress CIP Data available

ISBN: 0-304-32795-6 (hardback)
      0-304-32797-2 (paperback)

Typeset by Fakenham Photosetting Limited, Fakenham, Norfolk
Printed in Great Britain by Redwood Books, Trowbridge, Wiltshire

Contents

*Dedicated to
my parents and brother
and the three gurus:
David, Eric and Penny*

Acknowledgements

A fanfare for the makers: Homo Promos, Consenting Adults In Public, Outcast, Gay Sweatshop, Neti-Neti, Cwmni'r Gwir Sy'n Llechu, OutRage!, The Sisters of Perpetual Indulgence, ACT-UP London, the casts of *Glitter* and *Brite Lites*, University College of Wales Drama Department, Aberystwyth; Steve Cook for faith at Cassell; Adam Jeanes; Jim Hoggatt; Michael Wilcox; John Banks.

Preface

It's Cool to Be
an Artichoke

*December 1992. I sign the contract for this book on the floor of
the OutRage! office in the Lesbian and Gay Centre, Cowcross
Street, London. It's Worlds AIDS Day, and this year's theme is
Community and Commitment. OutRage! are planning to
demonstrate against the London Rubber Company, known as
producers of fine condoms throughout the world. Except for gay
men, that is. So, with helium-inflated condoms resting on the
ceiling, I grab a pen from my Commissioning Editor and sign a
contract for a book provisionally entitled* Striking a Pose *(not my
choice of title).*

*We loaded the inflated condoms into bin liners and
wandered off to the headquarters of the London Rubber
Company. We waited in a tube station for half an hour. I
wouldn't say we looked suspicious, but every now and then one of
the bin liners we were holding would levitate upwards as a
helium-filled condom battled for freedom.*

*The signal came to invade the offices. We missed them the
first time round and waited at a bus stop. And then we were in,
condoms out of the bags and whistles blowing. We infiltrated
every floor, and stuck placards in the window calling for extra-
strong condoms for anal intercourse. A couple of the group were
wearing condom costumes and did a little condom jig. We made
our point, and were given the sort of promises executives make to
get you out of their building.*

*There were at least two other authors on the newly
announced Cassell Sexual Politics list with me on the
demonstration, and my editor. I joked to him, 'Some wanker will
write a book on this sort of thing.'*

*And I thought, this is what we do now. These
demonstrations are part of how we live our lives these days.*

'Gay theatrical manoeuvres' was a term first put to me by Sister
Vicious Power Hungry Bitch, an American Sister of Perpetual
Indulgence who was over in Britain on a visit. The week before, he
had shocked a presenter on a local television programme in
Manchester by ripping up a page from a bible in front of the camera
(Vish confided in me that in fact he only ripped out a blank page,
but nevertheless got the reaction he wanted). Over tea and cakes,
we talked about how the gay community self-consciously uses
theatricality and ritual to celebrate and protest its existence. The
following day, World AIDS Day, we stopped traffic in Trafalgar
Square by sitting in the road. The police were frightened about
moving us on because there were a number of men wearing habits
and drag in the group. It was all a bit too *obvious*.

At the time I met Vish, I was busy doing research on gay
theatre for a postgraduate dissertation. Much has been written and
published on gay theatre since then, which is encouraging. My
research was proving frustrating, however – much of my own work
in theatre and as an activist seemed very far away from the characters and concerns in, say, Mart Crowley's *Boys in the Band*.
Whereas it was all very interesting to speculate on what characters,
authors or writers might be gay, or what the potential subtexts in
traditional texts might be, there seemed a lack of discussion on gay
theatre *practice* – how, why or where gay men produce theatre or,
more particularly, theatrical events.

Straight theatre celebrates and legitimizes its own street
theatre as a form, so that even the most amateur productions can be
analysed or reviewed. And the importance of community or political theatre has been well documented, and given particular emphasis in Europe with the fall of the Eastern bloc and the Berlin Wall.
Sister Vish told me how the Sisters were standing in full drag on
pillars as the Wall came down. 'They'd never seen anything like it,'

he boasted. And I thought, 'Mmmm, you're not wrong there. They have difficulty enough accepting that sort of thing in London.'

Summer 1988. Aberystwyth, Wales. My first gay theatrical manoeuvre. Elections for the student union were taking place, and an openly gay candidate was standing for the presidency. It was the time of Section 28, and bitter debates about that and the role of lesbian and gay rights in the Union's equal opportunities policies had made us the enemies of one of the all-male, rugby-shirt-wearing halls of residence. Come the election campaign, anti-gay posters were up on the hall windows.

And it was supposed to be our local polling station. So I went in drag with 'Sweet Transvestite' from the Rocky Horror Picture Show *blaring on a portable stereo. I cast my vote, threw down a bouquet of flowers, said hello to The Lads, and minced out to a waiting car. They sure as hell weren't going to intimidate me at the polling station.*

No, it didn't change the outcome of the election. (We lost, but did get the post of lesbian/gay officer into the constitution.) And, more satisfying, that particular hall was knocked down the following year and turned into a shopping arcade. There is a god.

I came out as gay in the shadow of a media backlash against AIDS, and during the campaigns which resulted in Section 28 of the Local Government Act. For many of us, Margaret Thatcher and her government were the impetus into not only gay politics but a particular form of rebellion against repression and coercion. Personally and politically, she is responsible for our need to watch our backs continually whenever gay rights are mentioned. Like some grotesque pantomime witch, she haunted and hunted down a generation of outcasts and castrated our dreams. The effects of her policies on social, political and sexual identities is irreversible; we have become her Frankenstein's monsters.

But, as they say in theatre, it's all a learning experience. In some way, it has to make us better people, if only to the extent that it makes us more determined to hold on to some of those cherished ambitions people call dreams. Many of us no longer want to – they're too hard, too idealistic, too impossible. And some of us still believe, in the way that people do believe these things, that there's always a fighting chance to change things for the better.

I write this only so that you know what I have at stake in all this. The notion of gay theatrical manoeuvres is part of an identity I grew up with. Or, more correctly, a series of identities which I've played with. And playing with identities, particularly (homo)sexual identities, is what this book is really about – how we find ways to play, and in turn a form of re-creation in the most literal and theatrical sense.

By the end of the 1980s, as Thatcher was facing her final comedown, a new set of identities was being seen in the gay community. We were all becoming, or being urged to become, *queer*. It was assertive, in-your-face radical chic, disabusing the negativity of media sloganizing around queers. It meant a fingers-up to the politeness of gay politics, and a petulant tantrum against the lack of basic civil rights for lesbians and gay men. Above all, it promised gay men and lesbians, people of colour, blacks, whites, straights, bisexuals, people with disabilities that we could all share an identity if we made ourselves different enough.

And many people objected, for all sorts of reasons: you can't reclaim the word 'queer'; queer is a form of internalized abuse; queer is an essentially American idea; queer is a commercialized fetishization of identity; despite claiming otherwise, queer is a legitimization for white middle-class gay men to dominate the political spectrum; queer only pretends to unite us all – in the end it either hides the differences between us or focuses them.

Very strong, (over-) dramatic positions began to be drawn. At one OutRage! meeting, a colleague threatened to burn himself if we didn't stop abusing him with the use of the word 'queer'. He'd actually brought the petrol with which to immolate himself if we didn't discuss his position. It was easy for us to joke about free barbecues, but also for many of us to secretly share his disquiet. On a lighter note, I wrote a letter to *Capital Gay* under my pseudonym as Sister Frigidity of the Nocturnal Emission:

Dear Editor,
I read with growing concern the ongoing debate over the use of the words 'Queer', 'Gay', 'Poof', 'Invert', and 'Big Girl's

Blouse' by militant lefty activists. Why, oh why, oh why do these troublemakers make T-shirts with such nasty and distasteful slogans, some of them using that naughty and impolite f-word?

I suggest that as homosexual people who are artistic and creative, we come up with a totally new word. My own favourite would be something which is tasteful and chic, such as 'Artichoke'. After all, like us, it's all heart. Let's see slogans like 'Out, Proud and an Artichoke', 'It's Cool to Be an Artichoke', and chants such as 'We're Here, We're Artichokes and We're Not Going Shopping.'

What a lovely mauve world it would be if we could all come out as Artichokes and put our hearts first.

And didn't some clever sod starting turning up to OutRage! meetings wearing purple T-shirts with 'It's Cool to Be an Artichoke', on. Still, it's more constructive than burning yourself alive.

These debates about identity and sexuality are historical, and so are our ways of creating and asserting them. Sexual identities aren't necessarily national identities, but identities reflect their time and place, and British sexual identities have always been intriguing and full of intrigue. They set us apart and bring us together, and so we devise ways to make them more immediate, more communal and inclusive in nature. And so we create, as part of this cultural exercise, theatrical manoeuvres which we hope will have resonance and meaning.

These things often go according to fashion or circumstance. Yet as we come to the end of the twentieth century, there's also a crisis in the terms and nature of our identities. National identities are losing their boundaries, class identities are losing their focus, sexual identities are losing their meaning. The danger of losing identity seems to be one of the worries of our time, and so it becomes dangerous to play with, confuse or muddle those identities. At the same time, such play allows us to become more constructive and open not only about what identities to choose, but what those choices of identities mean. And so it's nothing to be ashamed of.

The main body of this work concerns gay male identities. I deliberately chose to look at how gay men use theatrical manoeuvres, rather than how gay men and lesbians might be seen to practise them. There are, naturally, cross-over points, but it seems a disservice to gay men and lesbians to lump two separate traditions together too arbitrarily. And, particularly, the deconstruction of male sexual identities has a focus different from that of women, alongside a different position in the construction of social identities. And I leave off this work where I now begin it – with the point that different communities can work together in different ways, and the recognition of those differences make us stronger, not weaker.

Much of my focus has been on England, and particularly on London, reflecting my own and other prejudices. I have made no attempt to be more representative, simply on the grounds that these areas seem to be the ones I should analyse first. Perhaps (and I hope this will be the case) different traditions, rituals and theatrical manoeuvres might be analysed in the future – there is time enough for it.

I now see myself not as particularly gay or queer, but a *nellie queen*, which is something I used to get called at school anyway. It allows a lot of licence, and not much definition.

So it happened that Sister Belladonna was in his rubber habit and I was wearing my mini with fishnets, and we were having a pint with the regulars at the Coleherne in Earls Court. Exactly a year ago, we had first worn our habits at the same pub, to join a demonstration against the local police who'd raided the Coleherne and harassed customers a week before. And while we were supping our bevvies, a leather queen started chatting to us. All of a sudden, he burst into tears. 'Why me?' he asked. 'I must deserve it.' 'Bullshit,' we replied, bought him a drink and discussed the effects of moralizing and guilt around HIV with him. After drying the tears and a drink or two, like a phoenix he clambered on to a pool table used as a stage by a stripper earlier that evening. Once upon a time, the leather queen had been a drag performer, and he started to dance one of his routines. Salome could not have been more beautiful. So there were two gay male nuns and an ex-drag-queen, surrounded by butch leather clones. It may not have been Kansas, but it was some kind of home. Dolphins can swim, drag queens can dance, but we can all be heroes.

Stop Press

Coventry, May 1994

Happily, and not so happily, certain events run on before me. Amidst allegations of a homosexual affair between two senior Government ministers (whom, unfortunately, I can't afford to name), tawdry reports of MPs dying in states of spectacular and intriguing undress and the threat of prosecution for teachers who provide contraceptive information for under-age kids, two particular events affect this book.

A rally outside the Houses of Parliament during the Commons vote on the age of consent. Stonewall stewards warn us all to keep our voices down as we await the outcome – apparently, a couple of thousand queens singing 'Somewhere Over The Rainbow' is intimidation and is losing us votes. Euphoria dissipates into anger as the result is announced. The age of consent is lowered from 21 to 18. I feel sorry for a 17-year-old friend I saw earlier at the rally with his boyfriend. The previous week, he'd been suffering abuse from the lads at college. Today, it's democracy that tells him he's not good enough.

And earlier that week, film-maker Derek Jarman – described throughout this book as 'St Derek' – died. The Saint Is Dead, Long Live the Saint.

Introduction

No Word for Snow

The caged bird sings
with a fearful trill
of things unknown
but longed for still
and his tune is heard
on the distant hill
for the caged bird
sings of freedom.

> Maya Angelou[1]

The one duty we owe to history is to rewrite it.

> Oscar Wilde[2]

Mike: There's no word in the Irish language for what you were doing.

Wilson: In Lapland they have no word for snow.

> Joe Orton, The Ruffian on the Stair[3]

Off the page and onto the Heath

IN October 1990, the London-based theatre company Homo Promos produced Eric Presland's controversial play *Leather* at the Finborough Arms in Earls Court. With the area accommodating a sizeable gay population and one of the largest gay pubs, the Coleherne, round the corner, the Finborough Arms seemed an ideal venue for the production. The play itself explored the role of power and violence in gay men's personal, political and public lives, and how such power and violence might be used (and abused) by gay men and by society itself. *Leather* attracted large audiences, particularly drawing London's SM gay scene, who arrived costumed in their best leathers for the evening. After one performance early on in the run, as the cast and audience were enjoying a drink in the bar downstairs (which did not have a regular predominantly gay clientele), one group was approached by a customer of the pub. Hardly able to stand, he nevertheless graphically illustrated a theory he had on the extermination of homosexuals involving firearms and a wall. Eventually, after being petitioned by members of the cast, the bar manager reluctantly removed him. The rest of the play's run was haunted by anti-gay graffiti and intimidation. After the season had finished, the management of the Finborough Theatre received a complaint from the brewery (who actually owned the theatre), claiming that *Leather* had attracted an 'undesirable' (*sic*) clientele and damaged trade (!). Allegedly, the pub regulars had complained to the brewery. Homo Promos were later told by other sources that in reality the pub itself had very few 'regulars', and at least two of them were secretly regular patrons of the Coleherne![4]

The following year, the same company revived *TeaTrolley*, Eric Presland's re-working of *A Midsummer Night's Dream*. It was produced as an outdoor performance on Clapham Common, at midnight on Midsummer's Night. The play was originally presented by Consenting Adults in Public (CAIP) at the Edinburgh Fringe Festival in 1981, and produced the following year on Hampstead Heath, the gay cruising ground where the play itself is set. It heralded the start of an annual production on Hampstead Heath so that the 'Heath plays' became somewhat of an institution, some years attracting an audience of over a thousand. *TeaTrolley* itself – subtitled 'A Midsummer Night's Scream' – was based on a real, if improbable, event in gay history. During the early years of the Gay Liberation Front, members decided to 'convert' gay men cruising on Hampstead Heath to political action. As one member recorded:

3: No Word for Snow

We went to Hampstead Heath at the dead of the night to meet our brothers who use the area for cruising. We brought our stove and saucepan and made some coffee and then gave it out to everyone who wanted a drink and a talk.

'Mike', Camden Gay Liberation Front[5]

Written entirely in Shakespearean verse, *TeaTrolley* narrates the events which follow the arrival of Peascod, 'a wise fairy', and Orangeblossom – 'an impetuous young fairy', at a heath in London. Their mission, like that of GLF in the 1970s, is to supply the cruising gay men there with hot tea and to 'bring our joyous message to the Heath'.[6] The first visitors to the Heath that the radical gay fairies discover are two identically dressed moustachioed lovers, the 'two ice-cream clones' Pistachio and Neapolitano. The monotony of a monogamous relationship leads Pistachio to cruise on the Heath for 'too, too solid flesh', leaving his companion to his own devices. Their departure is followed by the arrival of the 'all leather-bound' Gaspatcho (*sic*), whose cruising codes and pressures dictate that he 'must not break the vow of Trappist silence' by speaking to other cruisers. After mischievously sending off the young Orangeblossom to talk with the midnight revellers, Peascod secretly adds a magic potion to the tea urn, with the intent that:

> The tea drinker shall on the instant fall
> Smitten by the object of desire
> On which his eye first lights.

The heady potion is drunk by characters as they chance upon the urn, and subsequently causes a series of improbable dalliances: Neapolitano falls in love with Orangeblossom; Constable Raspberry ('a fair and fruity cop' seeking to arrest cruisers on the Heath) sings lengthy love songs to Pistachio, who in turn falls back in love with Neapolitano; Gaspatcho breaks his traditional silence and gushes with love and admiration for Peascod, while Orangeblossom eventually sheds his high moral tone and begs Gaspatcho to 'tie me, bite me, beat me, whip me, fuck me'. In the final scene, Peascod stages events to illustrate the 'moral' that:

> truth is a plurality
> Not tolerance, or other liberal phrase,
> But taking each from each in richer ways.

Their follies have been cathartic – Constable Raspberry, liberated from his institutionalized bigotry, sees:

> that I have err'd in this alone,
> Hating in each other's hearts what's in my own;
> And I can never act fair or free
> While all that oppresses thee, oppresses me.

Similarly, Orangeblossom learns through his own (pleasurable) experience of sado-masochism and role-play that he must not be so quick to condemn others:

> For, in condemning their reality,
> I put down also what is part of me.

Neapolitano and Pistachio are reunited in a relationship based on mutual understanding and Gaspatcho finds that friendship is as enriching as sex.

The 1991 revival on Clapham Common found itself contextualized by a series of events which had nothing to do with the play text. In the few months leading up to the performance, several gay men had been attacked by 'queer-bashing' gangs while cruising on the Common, so that an assembly of lesbians and gays in the vicinity watching a play became a defiant act charged with significance. The self-styled queer activist group OutRage!, which had initiated several anti-queerbashing campaigns, was invited to attend the performance and sell whistles for protection. In addition, the site itself was situated in the middle of disputed ground owned by Lambeth (Labour-controlled) and Wandsworth (Conservative-controlled). While Homo Promos had been given permission to perform on the Lambeth ground, Wandsworth refused to allow a performance on their land, so that constant re-negotiating was needed to persuade audience members to remain on the 'right' (permitted) ground, approximately marked by the line of a group of trees. Given that the time of the performance was midnight, it proved to be a less-than-visible territorial marker. In addition, the Common's 'cruising ground' itself (an attractive feature that night) was in the Wandsworth half of the park.

These two examples of what might be called 'gay theatre' weave together both the *form* and the *content* of gay culture. While both plays are undeniably gay whatever the definition used (and, as will be examined later, there are many definitions which might be used), the context is peculiarly and identifiably gay. The various manifestations of intimidation and homophobia during the production of *Leather* made the Finborough Arms a set on which another (similar) drama about power, violence and control was being played out. The night-time antics of cruisers 'performing' elsewhere while *TeaTrolley* was being presented on Clapham Common were also part of the theatrical 'event'. The scripted play itself no longer dictated the action – indeed, the most dynamically theatrical performances on these two occasions were themselves unscripted but also a common factor in many gay men's everyday lives. There is nothing new in our having to confront homophobia and enact assertive strategies with which to confront such attitudes, or in practising the time-honoured ritual of cruising in public parks late at night. Or, for that matter, in gay men 'straight acting', passing for heterosexual, or camping around. Such events are part of the culture not only which we find for ourselves but also which we create for ourselves. Our social identities are to a large extent based on codes and rituals, different ways in which we act out our lives in public and private. If, as Judith Butler has claimed in *Gender Trouble*, gender is 'performative', the 'repeated stylization of the body, a set of repeated acts within a highly regulatory frame that congeal over time to produce the appearance of substance, of a natural sort of being',[7] then the emerging queer identity is self-consciously theatrical and performative, 'a world of possibility waiting to be explored'.[8] The new collective self-consciousness of performance reflects how, individually and collectively, we have frequently constructed theatrical manoeuvres to enable us to act our parts well.

Homosexual acts

In 1992, the professional theatre company Gay Sweatshop ran a series of workshops and discussions around aspects of gay theatre, entitled Queerschool. A panel of theatre practitioners, critics and academics gathered together to debate 'Queer Theatre' were forced to agree to disagree on a coherent definition or aesthetic which might be called 'queer theatre'.[9] Given the problematic history of 'gay drama', this is hardly surprising. If the very idea of a 'gay sensibility' might be seen as controversial, then any notion of 'gay theatre' – a theatrical aesthetic shaped by, for and about a nebulous gay consciousness – must be somewhere over the rainbow. The definitions used in the broad arena of gay drama are as various as the dramas they describe, and indeed the commentators describing them. Creating an aesthetic genre based on representations of (homo)sexuality is no less difficult than describing what homosexuality is, and simplifying definitions can lead to misinterpretation and a canon of works related only by what major or minor characters do or don't do in bed (on or off stage). In his introduction to the first British anthology of *Gay Plays*, editor and playwright Michael Wilcox states that

> This anthology has deliberately avoided plays that are concerned with gay politics. Here are not plays written by a minority for a minority audience. Each play stands with confidence and independence. None is an apologia for homosexuality.[10]

In her introduction to the sister collection, *Lesbian Plays*, Jill Davis takes a rather different position:

> The position from which I decided to put together a volume of lesbian plays is one which does claim that homosexuality is a political matter. It proposes that human sexuality is shaped by, and can be understood by reference to, the specific political and ideological system within which an individual is brought up. This is a view which rejects a

purely biological explanation of sexuality. It is what is meant by 'sexual politics', which is the political project of both the Gay and Women's Movements.[11]

The theatre critic Nicholas de Jongh, in studying the emergence of the homosexual on the modern (mainstream) stage in *Not in Front of the Audience*, chose to look at those plays which 'describe situations and pose moral dilemmas where homosexual desire, whether latent or manifest, precipitates a crisis'.[12] This approach, and de Jongh's general analysis, necessarily marginalizes those plays and theatre companies (many of whom produced pieces of theatre rather than written texts) which aren't approved by, or assimilated into, mainstream culture. The question of representation in theatre has been hotly debated, particularly around issues of class, gender and race, and finds a primary focus in the discussion of sexual identities. This discussion itself – who is represented and how – is mirrored in frequent debates within the gay community which continually has to pose the fundamental question of 'who are our elders?' and 'how do they assume/seize/are given control or authority?' The questions around 'gay drama' therefore become connected with questions around identity, presentation and representation, and demand that more convincing definitions must be discovered, or at least debated.

Don Shewey, in his introduction to a collection of British and American gay plays, *Outfront*, offers an important distinction which helps to narrow our focus: he makes a significant difference between 'gay theater' and 'the appearance of gay characters in mainstream plays'.[13] It is largely with the latter that most documentaries of the area have been concerned, perhaps indicating a conservative reluctance to negotiate the more problematic terrain of sexuality, identity and politics on and off stage. To reject the politics of gay drama completely is to claim that (homo)sexuality is not shaped by, or has a primary relationship with, society's material structures. Michael Wilcox's own experience of politically motivated theatre 'suggests to me for all the skill of the staging and the brilliance of many of the artists involved, political considerations seem to smother the more durable, dramatic instincts of most of the playwrights'.[14] The pressure here is to ensure that gay drama should transcend political rhetoric and reach out to a broader audience owing to the aesthetic quality of its art. But if there is no recognizable gay aesthetic, on whose terms is the aesthetic being dictated? Caroline Sheldon, writing about gay representation in film, has pointed out:

> The artistic sphere has long been claimed by gay men as legitimate territory; in this area the male homosexual has found the means to pass by identifying himself as artistic/romantic rather than be simply gay, so the social rejection on the basis of sexuality is re-focused by the justification of art.[15]

Michael Bronski, more critically, asserts in *Culture Clash* that because 'high culture' has an air of respectability, 'many gay men are drawn to it in order to cash in on that respectability', and quotes the gay slang term 'piss elegant' as a 'criticism of gay men who ape rather than reinvent the status quo'.[16]

We are also beginning to see in the different viewpoints that Wilcox and Davis put forward about what constitutes gay theatre a reflection of the two most dominant modern arguments about gay identity itself. Wilcox argues against 'any special pleading' (p. 8), and argues that our sexuality is equal to and as natural as heterosexuality, what might be termed as essentialist viewpoint of sexuality – sexuality is predetermined biologically. Jill Davis's viewpoint incorporates a line of thought much more closely aligned with the 'social constructionist' theory of sexual identity, where sexualities are given and attach to themselves meanings which are socially and historically determined. Jonathan Dollimore, in *Sexual Dissidence*, embodies the essentialist and anti-essentialist viewpoints respectively in describing a chance encounter between André Gide and Oscar Wilde in Algiers in 1895.[17] Wilde himself is the architect of sensibilities, while Gide or Dollimore becomes representative of the humanist and essentialist theories about identity and culture. But these questions are not simply an interesting historical or literary sideline. These questions of identity are intrinsically linked with who makes and controls 'culture', how it is defined and controlled and where it takes place.

9: No Word for Snow

The American writer Richard Hall, in 'The elements of gay theater', acknowledges the problems of defining 'gay theatre', but also acknowledges that 'what we are after is something new, not something old and borrowed'.[18] Hall goes on to identify four elements which he suggests are needed to create 'gay theatre'. He lists these as being community, identity, subject matter and audience. Any piece of gay theatre, he suggests, will acknowledge the fact of gay community, either explicitly or implicitly. For Hall, the obvious mirror of this is that such theatre will also acknowledge gay identity, 'a place where liberation is lived',[19] as an option in life. Hall also closely links sexuality with subject matter, welcoming the eroticization of gay sexuality on stage. Finally, Hall claims that the (gay) audience both supports and invents the text – knowing that there is a gay audience can help encourage writers in exploring gay themes and characters. These four regulations on what might be called gay theatre are useful in analysing what gay theatre consists of apart from just looking at homosexual characters or themes. It suggests that a radical gay theatre is something more than just a play which involves presenting homosexuality in some way. What is most interesting about Hall's categories is the way in which they cut across style or dramatic form, and do not simply claim 'camp' or 'irony' as a particularly gay sensibility. However, his essay – written in 1978 – also reflects the optimism and confidence of the strong and growing gay consciousness of the period.

Despite a large amount of work by gay writers, and plays with gay characters and themes, it would not be true to say that 'gay theatre' – in Hall's terms – has taken off. Gay theatre is allowed to make guest appearances in large theatres, more often on the fringe, and sometimes in community centres and schools. High-profile productions such as *Bent* by Martin Sherman and *Angels in America* by Tony Kushner have been staged to great acclaim at venues such as the Royal National Theatre. In London, a group of academics and theatre practitioners called Gays and Lesbians In Theatre (GLINT) has recently formed to look at the interests of lesbians and gays working in theatre, and to rise the profile of lesbian and gay theatre. These encouraging signs must, however, be weighed against the increasing inaccessibility of theatre and the arts, gross under-funding and such changing emphasis on the role of theatre and community arts as embodied in the National Arts and Media Strategy, moving away from the artist's right to fail to the artist's duty to experiment. All these events have an effect on lesbian/gay representation in the arts, particularly if it is to represent the challenges of an assertive post-Stonewall-riots liberation and identity. (We shall discuss Stonewall later.) It is worth, therefore, looking at one way in which Hall's criteria may be seen at work in a dynamic and creative relationship between theatre and the gay community.

Consenting Adults In Public

In December 1980, following Gay Sweatshop's temporary absence from the gay theatre scene as a result of losing its annual grant from the Arts Council, the Consenting Adults In Public (CAIP) drama group was formed. Drawing people from diverse backgrounds in response to advertisements placed in the lesbian and gay press, the group's name was chosen as a response to the infamous 1967 Sexual Offences Act, which resulted in the partial decriminalization of homosexual acts between two consenting men over the age of twenty-one in the privacy of their own home. CAIP set out, through 'collective working in a non-hierarchical way . . . to create an umbrella organisation with a political stress to the left, under which anything could happen'.[20] Theatre was seen as a way of 'helping people in the process of change', involving direct and reciprocal contact with the audience. The first organized events, in February 1981, were a series of workshops at the Thornhill Neighbourhood Centre in Islington, which were intended to 'go beyond skill sharing in a purely theatrical sense and could become a kind of consciousness raising, developing ideas and a sense of personal well being, self-confidence and gay pride'.[21] A series of 'Sunday Fundays' was also started at the Hemingford Arms pub, involving cabaret and play readings. The energy and enthusiasm generated from the early workshops led to three productions – *The Madness of Lady Bright* by Lanford Wilson, *Gas Man* by Alan Wakeman and *A Nice October Day* by Peter Robbins. *The Madness of Lady Bright*, together with Robert Patrick's *One Person*, and *See Saw*, *TeaTrolley* and *All Our Yesterdays* – all three written by CAIP founder Eric Presland – were taken to the Edinburgh Fringe Festival later that year.

The year 1981 had seen CAIP emerge and begin to establish itself as a community-based theatre group using, and performing to, members of London's lesbian and gay community. It was specific both geographically and in terms of its political and ideological make-up. Members of Outcast, which CAIP later became, used this to establish and define themselves as a community theatre group, with all the responsibilities (and difficulties) that this implies. The name Outcast asserted the group's primary relationship as being with the gay community, rather than mainstream society.

In many ways, the ideals and working practices of CAIP and Outcast represent a reconstituted social contract, a term redefined by Monique Wittig in 'On the social contract' as 'the fact of having come together, of being together, of living as social beings'.[22] The conventional social contract Wittig sees as that of 'living in heterosexuality'.[23] We are understood to be part of the social contract when we live heterosexually, i.e. when we date a partner of the opposite sex, marry and have children. This stands as a predetermined role which individual 'contractors' are urged to follow. As Rousseau himself implied when he talked of the social contract, it must be continually renewed and realigned in accordance with the wishes and needs both of the group and of individuals. Outcast, by definition, set up a new social contract. It is particular to their social role and function as a theatre company – 'People in the group come along to do a drama workshop – this, as it were, is the contract between us'.[24]

The idea of a new social contract enacted through drama is not new. The South American theatre practitioner Augusto Boal attempts in his work with disempowered communities to 'help the spectator to transform himself/herself into a protagonist of dramatic action' so that he/she can then extrapolate into his/her real life those actions he/she has rehearsed in theatrical practice.[25] Outcast took homosexuality as the basis for their new contract, and many of their ideas about the role of theatre are similar to Boal's. Empowering people on the basis of a fundamentally different contract creates possibilities for re-enacting the newly formed contract outside the drama workshop. The participants perceive themselves differently, outside the heterosexually constructed social contract. The new contract is reformulated according to their own wishes/ desires/needs, in the way it relates both to society as a whole and to other contractors. Furthermore, the importance of the contract being *social* is important for CAIP/Outcast's avowed aims as a theatre company:

> offering workshops for lesbian and gay people who are interested in all aspects of theatre and drama (movement, lighting, improvisation, etc.), and in using these aspects to look at our lives as lesbians and gays both in an individual and in a social/historical role.[26]

The last decade or so in Britain has seen an increasing 'privatiz- ation' of social roles and contracts, particularly noticeable in the effects of legislation on and attitudes to trade and political unions, leaving individuals disenfranchised – or 'opting out' – from the body politic. A social contract which involves groups of people collaborating and working together on a project which reflects a collective, rather than individual, identity has a particular import- ance for the visibility of lesbians and gay men. As the writer and theatre practitioner Neil Bartlett (himself a former administrator of Consenting Adults In Public) has pointed out: 'The fiction that we are hidden must first be constructed, so that when it is opportune or politically expedient to do so, we can be discovered'.[27]

The emergence of a lesbian and gay theatre group such as Outcast/CAIP is noteworthy for its discussions around lesbian and gay drama, broadening definitions of the genre from works based solely on lesbian/gay/homosexual characters to ones in which they interrelate as a community. The pioneering professional work of groups such as Gay Sweatshop is complemented by Outcast's work where none of its members can 'fail' because value judgements of the work are not the only – or most important – criteria. The productions are the visible end-product of a process which in itself is of great importance and relevance to those involved. The work- shops 'provide the atmosphere for people to stretch their limi- tations and boundaries'.[26] Having identified community as one reference point for gay theatre, Richard Hall points out that 'Gay theater will bear witness to some sort of community, to a shared experience of choosing sides, that is a central fact of gay life. Events onstage will be joined somehow to our choices offstage'.[29]

Anne Jellicoe, in writing about community theatre, asserts that 'Communities need community events to continually refresh them'.[30] This is particularly true for a lesbian and gay community where invisibility is constructed by moral and political forces to negate any sense of solidarity apart from our position as 'outsiders', preventing the private from going public. The denial of identity is as important for individuals as for communities – as Neil Bartlett writes, 'Wilde was not intolerable because he was a homosexual. He was intolerable because he was a public man who was a homosexual'.[31] Theatre, as the most public art form, is also the most dangerous in its presentation of the lesbian and gay community. It asserts and, through its audience, proves that such a thing exists. Community events, as Jellicoe indicated, are important for a sense of community – which is why we have Stonehenge, the Egyptian pyramids, the giant stone heads of Easter Island, the modern space programme and even the Channel tunnel. They all represent the community's achievements, while also helping to rebuild and reconstruct a community's identity, imbuing it with a sense of purpose. With drama, this produces a sense of collective and personal history, placing the lesbian and gay community in a context where its relationship with a social system constructed and dominated by compulsory heterosexuality is examined and subsequently challenged. The importance of Outcast's type of gay theatre lies in its ability to 'rescue imaginative space from the onslaught of heterosexual society'.[32] As the gay writer Edmund White has noted,

> A fantasist . . . sets herself or himself up as someone capable of re-imagining the world – and this challenge to order is perceived by cultural conservatives as 'wrong', dangerous, anomalous, decadent. The anomaly is that an individual is exercising the right to *play* in a state of complete freedom, and this exercise becomes an invitation . . . to live lives of freedom.[33]

Outcast set out to recreate community through a social contract specific to its theatre workshops, providing a controlled and protective environment in which members worked collectively to reclaim the tools of theatre in order to speak about their lives and interests, so that 'No one is going to claim to have their act together about me unless it involves me'.[34] What Outcast did in a confined space, and with a contract specific to the time and place, was to hold a rehearsal or playing out of alternatives, in the same way that many different groups now use theatrical techniques – for example Drama-in-Education in the classroom, role-play in assertiveness or management training, or participatory theatre in HIV/AIDS education. What we can see are some of the ways in which theatre and drama might be see not as high art, an end in itself, but as an art form – tools which can be used to create and affirm personal and social identities. And it is here that 'gay theatre' is most manifest and most successful.

Oscar Wilde was accused by the Marquess of Queensbury not of being a sodomite, but of 'posing as a somdomite' (*sic*). In other words, he was accused of acting out a transgressive identity. Legal and medical discourse have historically talked of 'homosexual acts'. During the 1970s, the gay liberation movement talked of coming out as a 'political act'. Famous homosexuals are 'unmasked' in public, over-wrought gay men are accused of 'making a scene' or being a 'drama queen'. In modern contact ads, many gay men boast of being 'straight acting'. Theatrical language has become enshrined in gay slang to become Polari, a secret (coded) language (see chapter 5). Theatricality and performance have been associated with the modern homosexual since the term was coined, and popular misconceptions of theatre see it as a business closely associated with, if not dominated by, homosexuals.

Theatre and theatricality have often been tools used to mask, encode and/or publicize (homo)sexuality, and it is in this respect that the connection between 'gay theatre', theatricality and gay – or, more recently, 'queer' – identity needs to be analysed more closely. Theatre and drama have not only been a means for homosexuals to 'pass' as sensitive or aesthetic, but have also been consciously used as a defence against and attack on compulsory heterosexuality and enforced gender codes. In his manifesto

Theatre of the Oppressed, Augusto Boal pays homage to the possibilities theatre can have as a weapon:

> For this reason the ruling classes strive to take permanent hold of the theater and utilize it as a tool for domination. In so doing, they change the very concept of what 'theater' is. But the theater can also be a weapon for liberation. For that, it is necessary to create appropriate theatrical forms. Change is imperative.[35]

What will be examined in the main body of this book are some of the ways in which gay men in Britain have adopted theatrical manoeuvres to create, affirm and protect sexual identities. 'Theatrical manoeuvres' can be defined most simply as the self-conscious and purposeful use of different forms of theatricality and ritual – in this context, particularly in regard to the presentation and representation of transgressive sexualities based on patterns of same-sex behaviour. While making use of appropriate texts and dramatic forms to help illustrate the theatrical nature of many of these manoeuvres, the main focus of discussion will be on more unconventional and immediate applications of theatre as an art form rather than a 'piss elegant' aesthetic. The examples already used – *Leather*, *TeaTrolley* and the work of Outcast/Consenting Adults In Public – cross over many of the traditional boundaries of theatre and drama, and serve as a meeting point between what has been discussed as 'gay theatre' and what I seek to define as gay theatrical manoeuvres.

The love that won't keep its big mouth shut

During 1991/2, I facilitated a series of interactive drama workshops on issues around HIV and AIDS.[36] The workshops were intended for health workers and youth workers, looking at ways in which drama techniques and conventions might be most effectively used in HIV education. The National AIDS Trust's Youth Initiative[37] in 1991 clearly highlighted interactive drama as one of the most direct and successful forums through which HIV education could take place. One particular workshop looked at the ways in which communities responded to the challenge of AIDS, and used brainstorming and role-play to create an entire fictional community. The group would be given a large sheet of paper with a main road on it, and asked to draw a map of their 'town', marking (and thereby placing) on the map the various resources which make a community – houses, shops, hospitals, pubs, churches, schools and so on. Once the 'community' itself had been created, participants would be asked to create characters for themselves within the town. The fictional characters need not represent the participants themselves in any way, and could be any age, race, gender, sexuality, occupation. The emphasis of the exercise was to examine a variety of people's attitudes, and participants were actively encouraged to examine situations different from their own. While many of the participants were willing to act out a different ethnicity, age, gender or religion from their own, gay men in the groups were willing to take on heterosexual, bisexual or gay roles (of both genders), but I noticed that the opposite was true of men who ordinarily identified as straight. In none of the groups I worked with did straight men act out a gay or bisexual role. Of course, within the terms of the workshop, this was not in any sense problematic or incorrect. But in the context of performative identities, I believe that the differences in attitudes are significant.

Of course, there are a variety of reasons why different decisions were undertaken, and what is being recounted is only an observation and not a controlled experiment. However, my own experience in the workshops suggested that gay men were more willing to (or more experienced in?) playing with sexual identities. *Submariners*, a play by Tom McClenaghan first performed at the Royal Court Theatre in 1980, is an unusual text in the way that it relates the story of a straight man pretending to be homosexual in order to escape from the military.[38] Set in a nuclear submarine, 'Cock' Roach assumes a gay identity in order to be dismissed from the navy, only to be approached by the end of Act One by a 'genuine' homosexual, Splash. Roach's own identity and his self-conscious play-acting are set up from the beginning of the play – one of his first actions is to flick through a 'girlie' magazine,

strongly marking him as heterosexual. In the play, his sexual identity is never really in doubt – the action concentrates on how far he
can 'take on' a gay identity as a theatrical manoeuvre in order to
achieve his ends. Once his play-acting becomes dangerous – when
fiction and reality cross over – he finishes the exercise. Splash, who
responds to Roach's advances, is established as married but 'really'
– that is, essentially – homosexual and so, in a very real way, acting
out different public and private sexual identities. Roach's sexuality
– naturally heterosexual – is never in question within the text, only
that of the transgressive, secretive Splash. Roach's theatrical
manoeuvres are an exercise and not a long-term strategy of survival
– he has the privilege of being able to play with an unconventional
identity in the short term, knowing that his heterosexuality will
enable him to renew his ordinary social contract at any time. He
can stop the game and reveal his 'true' identity as and when he has
achieved his goals. Splash, however, becomes an outsider *because*
he has slipped from his performative role, and revealed his 'true'
identity as homosexual. For the rest of the play, he is the 'outsider'.

The struggle for identity, and debates around 'true' and
imposed identities, have been at the centre of gay politics, and
particularly gay drama, for decades. The process of coming out, the
most literal realization or re-evaluation of sexual identity, has been
documented in many gay plays, most notably in Britain in Gay
Sweatshop's *Mr X* and its sister play *Any Woman Can*. Both plays
combine personal experience with the lesbian and gay movements'
'coming out' in British theatre in the 1970s. Both plays also reflect
the maxim that 'the personal is political' and that coming out is a
necessary politicization of the self, being both liberating and revolutionary. Although they are similar in style and content, I will look
more closely at *Mr X* in order to examine more thoroughly some of
the tensions involved in adopting an openly gay male identity.

Mr X by Roger Baker and Drew Griffiths (staged 1975)[39]
was based on the booklet *With Downcast Gays* by Andrew Hodges
and David Hunter, which explored how homosexual self-
oppression manifests itself in internalized homophobia. *Mr X*
records many of the experiences the members of Gay Sweatshop
themselves went through, and through a series of short scenes
traces the journey of Mr X, a gay Everyman, as he begins to come

to terms with this homosexuality.[40] The play begins with four
actors miming masturbation. It is at this stage that the young Mr X
realizes he is different from his peers – he is masturbating over Steve
McQueen rather than Raquel Welch or Brigitte Bardot. This
produces a hostile reaction from the others, whose abuse is echoed
in quotations from the Houses of Parliament. Mr X's confusion is
consolidated as a child at school by his teacher's naive and misleading lecture on sex and marriage. After the lecture, Mr X concludes
that 'I knew I wasn't normal and healthy because nothing of what
he said applied to me', and asks the question 'What do you do when
you find that you are the person you've been taught to despise?'
Looking for an answer, he turns to the Church, which rebaptises
him with a new and anonymous identity, launching him on a
journey through 'this vale of sorrow'. Like many of his contempor-
aries at the time, Mr X passes for straight at work, where he is
advised that 'having a wife gives a man something to work for' and
adopts the sexist colours of his workmates while praying 'Dear
God, please introduce me to another, just one other person like me'.
A flasher introduces him to the gay scene, whose inhabitants wait
dolefully in hope of an idealized 'husband' to lead them to happi-
ness, advertising in *Gay News* with an encoded jargon that reveals
more by its subtext than content, all for 'A small fee for the end of
my isolation'. A pseudo-marital relationship leads Mr X into Part
Six of the play, 'Catharsis', where a television interview puts him in
conflict with a Gay Rights activist, David, who points out to the
interviewer that he and Mr X are invited on the show only because
'we're both side-show freaks for your viewers to gawk at'. David's
advice to Mr X is that 'You get our own standards . . . Until you do,
you're fighting a battle you can't win because basically you're fighting yourself.' This pulls into focus Mr X's current relationship with
his lover, modelled on – and failing because of its definition by –
heterosexual marriages, resulting in him telling his would-be 'wife',
'I'd no idea you hated everyone and yourself so much'. Mr X's new-
found assertiveness and pride is put to the test by a sexist and racist
drag 'entertainer' who challenges him to come on stage:

This I have to hear. Ladies and Gentlemen – a homosexual

who hasn't got any problems. So *she* thinks! I can't wait for this. It's all yours, ducky. Do your worst.

The theatrical manoeuvre that follows is a defiant re-casting of Mr X not as a character in a play, but revealing the actor playing a part, asserting his homosexuality not as a mask adopted for the stage but as a positive and important part of his life off stage – 'No more split lives and dual personalities'.

Roger Baker, writing about *Mr X* in October 1984, points out:

> *Mr X* is very much a product of its time. Reading it again, almost ten years after it was written, it seems to recreate a world significantly different from that in which gay people live today. In many, many ways the lives of gay people are more comfortable today. But *Mr X* reminds me of what seems to have been lost: passion, discovery, that determination to take control of our own lives, and . . . maybe most important of all . . . a sense of the future.[41]

Mr X represents the fusing of Gay Sweatshop's personal and professional endeavours and the responses to it at its first performance at the 1975 Campaign for Homosexual Equality conference in Sheffield were enthusiastic, accepting it for what it was, 'primarily a piece of agit-prop for the Gay Movement . . . reaching out to people who were themselves Mr X's'.[42] Its Brechtian style made it a direct and challenging rallying call for the new gay consciousness, both terrifying and thrilling audiences with its unapologetic openness. It also marked a turning point for Gay Sweatshop:

> In many ways the five members of the company were like ambassadors for the Gay Movement and it was crucial that they were themselves gay. Through travelling around the country with the play, holding the discussions and providing *Gay News* and gay publications on a bookstall, the company became part of a network of information.[43]

Mr X is concerned with the possibility (and necessity) of change.

The central character is taught and encouraged to hide himself within a heterosexual and moralistic framework, but discovers this to be untrue; from his own experience, social order is constructed solely on misrepresentation and falsification. It's only when fear is challenged that the possibilities for liberation and freedom are seen. In existentialist terms, this consciousness or freedom to be whatever one chooses to be (Sartre's 'anguish') urges Mr X to reject his 'bad faith' (*mauvase foi*) and to be as sincere or authentic as he can be to his own individual identity. Mr X acknowledges the trauma and distress which brings him to this point of liberation, but rejoices in his own re-birth. It is here that *Mr X* shadows many of the tenets of 'catastrophist drama', most closely associated with Howard Barker's visionary drama of power and reconstitution of self and state, which David Ian Rabey defines as examining 'The aftermath of social disintegration and attempted restitutions of moral order'.[44] The search for identity, particularly a sexual identity, and how that identity is constituted and defined, is at the heart of Mr X's journey – until he announces that he is no longer playing a character but is in reality a gay actor, he has no name and, therefore, no identity. Dag Hammarskjöld, the reputedly gay UN secretary-general, referred more philosophically to the search for identity in his spiritual writings:

> At every moment you choose yourself. But do you choose *your* self? Body and soul contain a thousand possibilities out of which you can build many *I*'s. But in only one of them is there a congruence of the elector and elected. Only one – which you will never find until you have excluded all those superficial and fleeting possibilities of being and doing with which you toy, out of curiosity or wonder or greed, and which hinder you from casting anchor in the experience of the mystery of life, and the consciousness of the talent entrusted to you which is your *I*.[45]

This act of choice, and the potential for rehearsing identities, performing identified and/or changing identities have been central to the gay movement since the Stonewall riots of 1969, where a self-consciously assertive (even aggressive) identity was adopted by the gay community in response to continued intimidation by the police and gangland bosses of New York. The traditionally dispossessed drag queens, closet queens and cruisers of the Stonewall Inn acted out their anger and frustration with police intimidation in three days of rioting and violent carnival. Performance was integral to the event and to a sense of an emerging community, to the extent that drag queens performed high-kick dance routines and musical numbers even as the rioting continued. The event itself has been immortalized in gay dramas such as *As Time Goes By* (produced by Gay Sweatshop in 1977) by Noël Greig and Drew Griffiths and *Street Theater* (1982) by American playwright Doric Wilson. In *Street Theater*, we see the fusing of fact and fiction as two of Mart Crowley's apolitical characters from *The Boys in the Band* (1968), Michael and Donald, stand and watch the momentous events. It is their cowardice and hypocrisy about their sexuality which force the closeted Sidney into action at the end of the play and give it its final and dramatic denouement:

> Donald: You faggots are revolting.
>
> (Sidney, horrified at Donald, makes his decision, tosses his sunglasses in the gutter, joins Ceil and the others.)
>
> Sidney: (To Donald and Michael) You bet your sweet ass we are!
>
> (Sidney, Ceil, Boom Boom, C.B., Heather, Jack, Timothy, Jordan and Gordon make a grouping worthy of a statue in Sheridan Square. Again flashing red lights illuminate the stage, accompanied by sirens.)
>
> Blackout[46]

Street Theater presents the audience with a mix-and-match group of lesbians and gays acting out an identity as a community – a community of outsiders who themselves have excluded and made outsiders of Donald and Michael. The binary opposition of the phrase 'out' – in order for something to be outside, there has to be something inside – is of particular interest and relevance in debates around sexual identity. Homosexuality and heterosexuality depend upon their existence as opposites of each other, exclusive categories which support, in fact create, each other's existence by necessitating each other. As Diana Fuss has pointed out in 'Inside/out':

> Paradoxically, the 'ghosting' of homosexuality coincides with its 'birth', for the historical moment of the first appearance of the homosexual as a 'species' rather than a 'temporary aberration' also marks the moment of the homosexual's disappearance – into the closet. That the first coming out was also simultaneously a closeting; that the first homosexual's debut onto the stage of historical identities was as much an egress as an entry; and that the priority or 'firstness' of homosexuality, which preceded heterosexuality in Western usage by a startling eleven years, nonetheless could not preempt its regulation to secondary status: all these factors highlight, in their very contradictoriness, the ambiguous operations of ins and outs.[47]

Fuss goes on to analyse the self-conscious use of 'out' as an identity, meaning both to be openly gay and out of the closet, but also to be on the inside, 'inside the realm of the visible, the speakable, the culturally intelligible'.[48] To act out an identity, to use theatrical manoeuvres to create and sustain cultural alternatives, will often mean complicating or confusing binary oppositions. The rise in the 1990s of 'queer politics', where the label 'queer' reflects any and all marginalized identities, or no identity, or 'any free-thinking, gender-liberated Gay, straight, Bi-sexual or Transgender person',[49] certainly reflects this attitude, even if it is not an entirely successful tactic or policy. The complex forces which shape sexuality, gender and sexual identity are in this study taken to be largely socially constructed, so that a trans-historical identity of 'homosexuality' is inaccurate and inappropriate. The fashionable use of the modern-day 'queer' is not something I wholeheartedly welcome, but I acknowledge it as part of a process of continuing redefinition, and it is useful for my purposes where 'queer' is taken to be associated largely with transgressive same-sex behaviour rather than homogenizing homosexuality as a single identity. Here, then, queer is a process of changing identities, looked at from a (post)modern perspective, which help to inform and shape our own present performative sexual identities. If the love that dares not speak its name has become the love that won't keep its big mouth shut, then it's also speaking different languages.

Acting out

The following chapters examine some of the ways in which gay men in Britain have adopted theatrical manoeuvres to create, affirm and protect sexual identities. 'Theatrical manoeuvres' I have tried to define as the self-conscious and purposeful use of different forms of theatricality and ritual, in this context particularly in regard to the presentation and representation of transgressive sexualities based on patterns of same-sex behaviour.

The broad scope of the book is to investigate and celebrate the different and imaginative uses of theatrical manoeuvres in gay subculture, and its challenge(s) to mainstream culture. Although my focus is firmly based in the present, I also look at how identities have been created and changed, and how 'theatrical manoeuvres'; have been manipulated in the past, in an attempt to point to ways in which they might be used in the future.

I have already looked briefly at some of the questions around identity and theatricality. The main body of the book is divided into three areas, looking more closely at theatrical forms or conventions, and how they have been adopted, or can be related to the idea of 'theatrical manoeuvres'. Although for the purpose of this book I have chosen to work under these sub-divisions, they are by no means exclusive, and forms, events and groups may appear and re-appear across the arbitrary and artificial divisions I have made use of.

First, the body. I intend to look at ways in which the body has become theatricalized, or defined as the ultimate space in and on which real dramas have been realized. The body makes manifest the homosexual/gay/queer and so often becomes the critical performance space. It is the physicalization of queer sexuality which makes it both visible and vulnerable. The human body is the stage on which sexual identities have meaning and are most fully realized, and can be the point at which difference is acknowledged or hidden, depending on what strategy is being pursued and by whom. On one level, I will look literally at bodies who have been associated with queer history, some of our most famous/celebrated/infamous 'actors' or 'performers', including Oscar Wilde and Joe Orton. In different ways and at different times they have been important public bodies who have been identified with changing ideas of sexual identity and have all acted out roles to shock, disturb or challenge. Following the idea that the physical body can itself be a playground for acting out different identities or possibilities, the most transgressive or disturbing theatrical manoeuvre adopted by gay men has often been seen to be cross-dressing or 'gender-fuck', where the body becomes the site for questions around sexual identity, gender and what Marjorie Garber has termed 'cultural anxiety'.[50] Finally, the collective and individual queer body has become the stage for what have variously been dangerous, inspiring or crucial theatrical manoeuvres in the face of the HIV pandemic, where responses to the AIDS crisis have not only shaped sexual identities and practices but have tested our ingenuity, anger and passion.

Second, semiotics. The history of queer sexualities has largely been one of encoded signals, where meaning can be read only by those on the inside. Gay semiotics have been used as a defensive and protective measure, often signalling contradictory or confusing messages which can be correctly decoded only with the help of certain information or experiences. The codes used may have hidden queer sexuality from public recognition, or they may have been used as shorthand for a range of gay histories. Complex and detailed codes have been worked out verbally and visually to relay a whole series of meanings not readily apparent. The fusion of languages to create Polari, a coded gay slang, is one theatrical manoeuvre where artificial forms of communication have been created for specific purposes, in this case to prevent heterosexuals listening to the 'dirt being dished' by groups of 'omipalones'. In modern times, fetishes can be signalled by complex hanky, key or bootlace codes, providing a sexual shorthand for cruisers. Camp, in many ways the ultimate queer code, is a complicated use of theatricality and style to hide – or often to deconstruct – meaning, and has been used to great political effect in the last decade by direct action groups such as ACT-UP and OutRage! in Britain.

Third, space. Changing sexual identities have been accompanied by a changing use of spaces, legally and illicitly appropriated and/or seized. Early modern history saw the creation of the private clubs or molly houses, with elaborate customs and rituals based on gender inversions and theatricality, while in the late nineteenth century homosexuality increasingly became a matter of public debate and scrutiny. Increasing pressure after the Wolfenden report in the late 1950s led to the 'privatization' of homosexuality with the 1967 Sexual Offences Act, but also ultimately resulted in the present public displays of the annual Gay Pride marches and festivals, and the more assertive and political theatrical manoeuvres of groups such as the Sisters of Perpetual Indulgence, OutRage! and ACT-UP. The growth of gay clubs, pubs, bookshops and meeting places has also changed the nature of spaces available, while semi-secret cruising grounds still provide room for a whole series of theatrical manoeuvres and rituals. By looking at the different possibilities which changing spaces provide for everyday theatricality and ritual, it is hoped that imaginations might be liberated and that familiar spaces and routines become complicated playgrounds where possibilities can be explored and boundaries pushed further and further back. The rise of direct action in queer politics has shown how the most mundane activities can become potential areas of conflict and possibility, where the most active imaginations can create and re-create radical potential and change spectators into protagonists, if not heroes.

Notes

1. Maya Angelou, 'Caged Bird' from *And Still I Rise* (Virago, 1986).
2. 'The critic as artist', in *The Complete Works of Oscar Wilde*, introduced by Vyvyan Holland (Book Club Associates, 1980), p. 326.
3. Joe Orton, *The Ruffian on the Stair*, in *Orton – The Complete Plays* (New York: Grove Weidenfeld, 1976).
4. *Leather* was produced at the Finborough Arms in October 1990. In 1992, the brewery became the centre of another dispute when it banned another gay play by the theatre company Starving Artists.

The same brewery, Whitbread, was also accused of homophobia during its 1989 billboard campaign for Flowers Bitter which used the slogan 'Not All Flowers Are Pansies'.

5. 'Midnite on Hampstead Heath', in *Come Together – The Years of Gay Liberation 1970–73*, ed. Aubrey Walter (GMP, 1980).

6. All references to the unpublished script of *TeaTrolley* by Eric Presland. Special thanks to Eric for making this available.

7. Judith Butler, *Gender Trouble: Feminism and the Subversion of Identity* (Routledge, 1990), p. 33.

8. 'I hate straights', anonymous pamphlet distributed in New York, cited by Keith Alcorn, 'Queer and now', *Gay Times*, issue 164 (May 1992).

9. 'Queerschool' Cocktail Seminar, 2 September 1992, at the Holborn Centre for Performing Arts in London. Panellists included writers Neil Bartlett and Andrew Alty, critic Paul Burston and photographer Della Grace, amongst others.

10. Michael Wilcox, Introduction to *Gay Plays*, vol. 1 (Methuen, 1984), p. 6.

11. Jill Davis, introduction to *Lesbian Plays*, vol. 1 (Methuen, 1987).

12. Nicholas de Jongh, *Not in Front of the Audience: Homosexuality on Stage* (Routledge, 1992), p. 3.

13. Don Shewey, introduction to *Outfront: Contemporary Gay & Lesbian Plays* (New York: Grove Press, 1988), p. 3.

14. Wilcox, introduction to *Gay Plays*, vol. 1, p. 7.

15. Caroline Sheldon, *Gays and Film* leaflet, British Film Institute, 1987.

16. Michael Bronski, 'The making of gay sensibility', in *Culture Clash: The Making of Gay Sensibility* (Boston: Southend Press, 1984).

17. Jonathan Dollimore, 'Wilde and Gide in Algiers', in *Sexual Dissidence* (Oxford: Oxford University Press, 1991).

18. Richard Hall, 'The elements of gay theater', in *3 Plays for a Gay Theater* (San Francisco: Grey Fox Press, 1983).

19. Hall, 'The elements of gay theater', p. 155.

20. Unpublished history of Consenting Adults in Public/Outcast Theatre Company. Thanks to Jane Hanna and Outcast Theatre Company for making this available.

21. CAIP/Outcast unpublished history.

22. Monique Wittig, 'On the social contract', in *Which Homosexuality?*, ed. Dennis Altman (GMP, 1989), p. 244.

23. Wittig, 'On the social contract'.

24. Outcast 'Guidelines' free handout.

25. Augusto Boal, 'The Sartrouville Experience', in *Theatre Papers*, no. 1. (Darlington College of Arts, Department of Theatre).

26. Outcast, 'Guidelines' leaflet.

27. Neil Bartlett, *Who Was That Man?: A Present for Mr Oscar Wilde* (Serpent's Tail, 1988).

28. Outcast publicity leaflet.

29. Hall, 'The elements of gay theater', p. 153.

30. Anne Jellicoe, *Community Plays* (Methuen, 1987), p. 46.

31. Bartlett, *Who Was That Man?*, p. 148.

32. Shewey, *Outfront*, p. xxiii.

33. Cited in Shewey; source: John Hofsess, 'Portraits of the artist: why is gay art gay?', *New York Native*, 20 December 1982.

34. Outcast publicity leaflet.

35. Augusto Boal, *Theatre of the Oppressed* (Pluto Press, 1979), p. ix.

36. Workshops based on Action AIDS techniques, resource pack published by Hodder & Stoughton.

37. *Living For Tomorrow*, The National AIDS Trust Youth Initiative, 1991.

38. Tom McClenaghan, *Submariners*, in *Gay Plays*, vol. 1, ed. Wilcox.

39. References to *Mr X* by Roger Baker and Drew Griffiths, unpublished script. Thanks to Gay Sweatshop for making this script available.

40. Philip Osment's history of Gay Sweatshop, 'Finding room on the agenda for love', in *Gay Sweatshop: Four Plays and a Company* (Methuen, 1989). Osment gives a full account of how *Mr X* was written and produced.

41. Roger Baker in a flyer for the Gay Sweatshop Times Ten Festival, 1985.

42. Cited in Osment, 'Finding room on the agenda for Love', p. xx.

43. Osment, p. xxiii.

44. David Ian Rabey, *Howard Barker: Politics and Desire* (Macmillan, 1989), p. 292.

45. Dag Hammarskjöld, *Markings*, translated by W. H. Auden and Leif Sjöberg (Faber & Faber, 1966), p. 38.

46. Doric Wilson, *Street Theater*, in *Outfront*, ed. Shewey, p. 77.

47. Diana Fuss, 'Inside/out', in *Inside/Out: Lesbian Theories, Gay Theories*, ed. Diana Fuss (Routledge, 1991), p. 4.

48. Fuss, p. 4.

49. Definition given in press release, 'Queer holy war', Sisters of Perpetual Indulgence Inc. (San Francisco), 16 January 1992.

50. See Marjorie Garber, *Vested Interests: Cross-Dressing & Cultural Anxiety* (Routledge, 1992).

Part One
The Body

Chapter one

Singing the Body Electric

*Where new possibilities in performance are being explored
around bodies and pleasures the rallying point remains
situated not with any conventional bodies, but more or less
in extremis those of feminists and gays, who are
deconstructing and recoding the ideology of gender.*

Herbert Blau,
To All Appearances: Ideology and Performance[1]

*There were things that heterosexual culture wanted from
Rock Hudson's body (a safe date was one) but only under
the proviso that the homosexuality underwriting those
things remain unspoken and precisely unspeakable.*

Richard Meyer, 'Rock Hudson's body'[2]

IN 'The queen's throat: (homo)sexuality and the art of
singing', Wayne Kestenbaum suggests that 'voice culture (and, by
extension, operatic singing itself) is inseparable from nineteenth-
and twentieth-century discourses of the sexual body, a choral
entanglement in which "homosexuality" was a major though taci-
turn player'.[3] The connection between homosexuality and its physi-
cality in the body – in a collective and subjective sense – is localized

in Kestenbaum's thesis in the throat, the physical area and the singing and erotic spaces it represents:

> the homosexual body, whether silent or vocal, occupies a crossroads where anatomies and institutions collide. Like voice, homosexuality appears to be taking place inside a body, when really it occurs in a sort of outerspace (call it a 'discourse') where interiorities converge; the vocal body and the homosexual body each appear to be a membraned box of urges, when actually each is a looseleaf rulebook, a ledger of inherited prohibitions.[4]

These illusions and contradictions of what is constructed as 'voice' or 'homosexual' are in sharp contrast to earlier theories about the connection between the (physical) body and the (homo)sexual. Physical characteristics defined queer sexuality so that it could be investigated, castigated and – most importantly – *recognized*. Dr La Forest Potter, in 1933, theorized that physical signs denoted the average homosexual, including large, easily aroused nipples, sloping and rounded shoulders, abnormally wide hips and 'feminine buttocks', and a mincing walk.[5] Today, some of these types of 'mannerisism' popularly attached to homosexuality have been adopted and/or subverted in self-conscious parody, for example the 'mincing machine' tour and antics of comedian Julian Clary. The body, in definition and meaning, has changed and changing meanings so that – far from being the physical, essential, ontological site of sexuality – it has become (or has always been?) part of the discourse.

It is perhaps with a sense of irony, then, that gay liberationists and moral reformers alike have pointed to the body as the battleground for sexuality and perversion. Historical figures are reclaimed or censored on grounds of sexuality, and modern debates around sex and sexual practice either welcome the body as the site of erotic possibilities or abhor its corruption and disease. Within the realm of theatre, the body too has a special significance. Actors and theatre practitioners can see the body as the essential (unique) tool of a performer (as in physical theatre, mime and dance) or displace it entirely with puppetry, shadow-play and voice or sound.

Starting with the historical body – in this case, the transgressive writers (performers) Oscar Wilde and Joe Orton – chapters 1–3 will examine how different concepts of the 'body' can be self-consciously theatricalized and subverted. Wilde and Orton, aside from creating performative identities for themselves, em-body important changes in the history of sexuality. Drag, where the individual body becomes a complicator of gender and sexual identity, has long been seen as the canvas for cultural anxieties around sexuality, and will be examined here within its peculiarly British tradition. Finally, the physical and social effects of the retrovirus that has come to dominate the last decade will be seen in the light of actions around, and reactions to, the AIDS crisis.

Oscar Wilde

Oscar Wilde's colourful life was an elaborate drama, often created but not altogether controlled by Wilde himself. It is easy to see Wilde's life in hindsight as a singular narrative with an inevitable 'conclusion', but it was Wilde's ability to surprise and confuse which made him such an enigmatic character, and which maintains our interest in him today. Artifice, or invention, helped him to create an aesthetic – and an identity – which bought him considerable success. It was only when he was accused of acting – of posing as a sodomite – that Wilde's downfall came about. As Michael Bronski has pointed out, 'if people "pose" (i.e. be other than who they are supposed to be) the structures of society are threatened'. In Wilde's case, his moral and artistic behaviour were seen as one and the same, because – according to Jonathan Dollimore – 'of a perceived connection between his aesthetic transgression and his sexual transgression'.[7]

Wilde's own theatrical manoeuvres included his flamboyant clothes – *The New York Times* described him in 1882 as 'dressed as probably no grown man in the world was ever dressed before'[8] – and his renowned wit. His own ideas on theatre and art in general were also carefully constructed to accord with his own behaviour; his love of beauty, a penchant for blue and white china or green carnations, all tied into his ideas of artifice and invention. Wilde, according to Neil Bartlett, had:

modelled himself on the liars, the comedians, the critics –
'the fool, the fraud, the knave' – anyone who had signed no
contract with truth; the embroiderers and inventors of the
truth, the prostitute. *He was entirely lacking in wholeness
and completeness of nature.* [Bartlett's emphasis][9]

Wilde's ability to 'create' a character was proved when, after being
released from Reading Gaol on 19 May 1897, he 'became'
Sebastian Melmoth, forging a new identity for himself. His reincar-
nation was another manoeuvre to protect himself and cover his
tracks,. leaving Bartlett to conclude, and celebrate the fact that
Wilde's ' "private" homosexual life was an elaborate drama of
deception, lies and, most of all, inspired invention'.[10]

Wilde's persona has come to mean, to embody, much more
than his own life. His trial was the result of several events during
the middle and later part of the nineteenth century. The categorization of sexuality saw the term *homosexualität* first coined by the
Swiss doctor Karoly Maria Benkert in 1869, and writings on
(homo)sexuality by such people as Richard Krafft-Ebing, Karl
Heinrich Ulrichs, Edward Carpenter, Havelock Ellis and J. A.
Symonds. Meanwhile, the publication of *The Origins of the Family,
Private Property and the State* by Engels in 1884, and the activities
of the German Social Democratic Party, affected public discourse
on the role of the family, and construction of sexuality. In novels
such as the confessional *The Sins of the Cities of the Plain*, or *The
Recollections of a Mary-Anne* (1881), homosexuality was treated
with more openness, and homosexual subtexts can be seen in such
plays as Arthur Law's *The New Boy*, staged in 1894, and in
another play of that year, *The Blackmailers* by John Gay and Marc-
André Raffalovich.

Times were changing. In the newly formed German states,
paragraph 175 of the penal code made all sex between men –
except for mutual masturbation – illegal. A series of legal changes
was brought about in Britain which saw the re-territorialization of
sexual practice and its control. By 1861, with the Offences Against
the Person Act, the death penalty for sodomy was replaced with
penal servitude, between ten years and life. Although the original
aim of the 1885 Criminal Law Amendment Act was to 'make

further provision for the protection of women and girls, the suppression of brothels and other purposes', Henry Labouchère added an amendment, later to become known as Labouchère's Amendment. Passed late at night on 6 August 1885, the amendment made all homosexual acts illegal:

> Any male person who, in public or private, commits, or is a party to the commission of, or procures or attempts to procure the commission by any male person of an act of gross indecency with another male person, shall be guilty of a misdemeanour, and being convicted thereof shall be liable at the discretion of the court to be imprisoned for any term not exceeding two years, with or without hard labour.

The effect of the law was to make it much easier to prosecute homosexuals. The Labouchère Amendment made no reference to the 1861 Act, and by 1898 the Vagrancy Act had also made homosexual 'soliciting' illegal. Lesbian sexuality was ignored, and failed to be included in the Criminal Law Amendment Act even after an attempt in 1921 to include it within those provisions. Fear that legislating against the act itself would produce greater knowledge about lesbianism was the basis of throwing out the proposition.

Before Wilde himself was brought to trial, there had been a number of homosexual scandals and trials. On the night of 28 April 1870, Mrs Fanny Winifred Park and Stella, Star of the Strand, were arrested after attending the theatre and charged with having committed the misdemeanour of being men and dressed in female attire. The case against Fanny and Stella – also known as Frederick Park and Ernest Boulton – attracted much attention, and is of interest for several reasons. Medical evidence was asked for to prove a charge that Boulton and Park were sodomites. However, the police surgeon could not tell if dilation of the anus was proof of sodomy because, after examining Fanny and Stella, he could only exclaim that he had seen nothing like it before. But Fanny and Stella weren't just dressed for the night – Stella lived with Lord Arthur Clinton M.P. as his mistress, and both Fanny and Stella had careers as actresses; in 1869, they had toured melodrama and one-act operettas to great acclaim. The trial began to centre on the couple's visibility, on the point that the crime of sodomy was essentially a furtive act and so the defence could prove that by their blatant exhibitionism, Fanny and Stella were not guilty as charged. When the jury agreed and Fanny and Stella were declared not guilty, Fanny fainted in the dock. As Neil Bartlett, whose researches brought Fanny and Stella to light, has remarked: 'Only by silencing, not punishing, the sodomites, could the court breathe a sigh of relief. When Boulton and Park were dismissed, declared improbable if not impossible, the existence of a homosexual culture in London was effectively denied'.[11]

In 1884, a scandal involving high-ranking officials in Dublin Castle once more brought up publicly the issue of homosexuality, and in 1889–90 the Cleveland Street scandal involving telegraph boys and a homosexual brothel, hinting at the involvement of Prince Albert Victor (son of the Prince of Wales) brought allegations of a cover-up operation prompted by the government. Thus, when Wilde's trial came about in 1895, implicating the current Prime Minister Lord Rosebery in the scandal – Rosebery had favoured the Marquess of Queensbury's eldest son – there was a very wide concern that the court should not be seen to be shielding those with privilege.

By 1895, Oscar Wilde was very well established in the public sphere. *The Picture of Dorian Gray* and *The Importance of Being Earnest* had ensured him an enviable reputation as a documenter of social masks and manners, a reputation he carried with wit and style into his own public appearances. 'Most of his work is concerned with the contradiction between moral standards and mundane reality,' Jeffrey Weeks has noted, while '*The Importance of Being Earnest*, his most enduring achievement, is above all about the double life'.[12] The play, concerning the exploits of two fashionable young men acting out different identities in the country and in London, has been re-interpreted by Neil Bartlett:

> When Wilde dedicated *The Importance of Being Earnest* as 'A Trivial Comedy for Serious People' he was dedicating it to us, since we too, in all seriousness, wish to order the world so that the financial is trivial, pleasure is without cost, lies and deceptions without punishment.[13]

37: *Singing the Body Electric*

The Importance of Being Earnest was premiered on St Valentine's Day, 1895. On 1 March Wilde set in progress a warrant for the arrest of the Marquess of Queensbury, the father of his lover Lord Alfred Douglas, whom Wilde affectionately referred to as 'Bosie'. Queensbury was infuriated by Wilde's relationship with his son and, in a letter to Wilde at his club, addressed Wilde as a 'posing somdomite' (*sic*), a charge Wilde took to be libellous. In the following court action, Wilde's literature and public and private life came under scrutiny – 'all his letters, stories, his novels, plays and poems now "meant" just one thing; they collapsed into a single, horrible text'.[14] Queensbury was vindicated and Wilde pilloried, a prosecution against him condemning him to the maximum penalty available for having 'been the centre of a circle of extensive corruption of the most hideous kind among young men'[15] – imprisonment and hard labour for two years. After the trial, Wilde's name was removed from publicity boards for the two theatres where his current plays – ironically, *An Ideal Husband* and *The Importance of Being Earnest* – were showing, although soon both plays were withdrawn, and plans for *A Woman of no Importance* to be toured in America were cancelled.

The effects of Wilde's trial were far-reaching. The fetishization of (homo)sexuality led to its denunciation but also to its acknowledgement. Wilde's downfall led to individuals identifying themselves as homosexuals, constructing elaborate communities and, ultimately, to creating reform organizations. 'The love that dare not speak its name' – which Wilde had himself denied – became public, but castigated. The net of silence had been broken. In future, Wilde's plays and works would be associated with a known homosexual, references would be seen in a different context. The categorization of homosexuality was part of the new order being structured around the industrialization of western capitalism, leading to a division between public and private roles and duties. Wilde's trial proved that the alienating categorization of homo- and heterosexualities led to a dichotomy; while homosexuality was made out to be the private practice of a few 'deviants' and not associated with the normative sexuality of the majority, its public disclosures also had profound implications for social mores and structures:

Wilde's transgressive aesthetic simultaneously confirmed and exploited this inextricable connection between the sexual and the (apparently) non-sexual, between sexual perversion and social subversion, and does so through Wilde's own version of that connection – 'what paradox was to me in the sphere of thought, perversity became to me in the sphere of passion' (Wilde, *De Profundis*, 466).[16]

The legacy of Wilde's theatricality and self-conscious posturing was that he uncovered a sham. The 'privacy' of sexuality was plainly a nonsense – the law was now constructed to 'make vice criminal: a man's acts are governed, and his character is moulded, by incentives to virtue, and the checks which hold him back from vice'.[17] The law emphasized that sexual patterns of behaviour affected the way that society operated. Not only this, but art and its possibilities were also seen as potentially threatening: Bronski, in *Culture Clash*, acknowledges our inheritance from Wilde:

> By arguing that art needed no reason beyond itself to exist, he was making a radical statement; art, form, style and 'posing' all existed outside of accepted social and moral codes. Their value was intrinsic, their power was that they represented an alternative and a threat to those codes.[18]

Wilde was not the only victim of the new attitudes towards homosexuality, simply the most public – a position that he himself had written and created for himself. Although his position now seems to embody all that was hypocritical about society's Victorian attitudes around sexuality, his transgressive posturings are also significant in reference to his place in society – exoticized and, despite his wit and creative genius, ultimately shunned and castigated.

The Oscar Wilde of welfare state gentility – Joe Orton

Orton assumed the mantle of Wilde's notoriety in the 1960s, often consciously referring to and subverting Wilde's own reputation. In many ways, however, Orton became the antithesis of Wilde, Oscar Through the Looking Glass. Wilde's effeminacy and dandiness were despised and spurned by Orton, who chose to create his own image as that of the phallic male, the working-class lad, the bit of rough. His T-shirt, jeans, leather jacket and boots replace Wilde's aestheticism as symbols and codes for a (homo)sexual costume, complicating and confusing predominant ideas in the late 1950s and 1960s about queers and pansies. Where Wilde relied on manners, politeness and *passing* through his knowledge of, and association with, the dominant class, Orton consciously challenged and outraged those sensibilities, even though he was ultimately reliant on them for his success as a playwright. As Simon Shepherd has pointed out in his radical reassessment of Joe Orton and his lover Kenneth Halliwell, *Because We're Queers*, Orton's act as working-class hero, a 'sexy hooligan', was constructed to cover the contradictions in his own life between radical ideology and practice:

> The problem that he could not resolve socially or economically could be *temporarily* solved in sex. He could act the working class lad and indulge in a form of sex distasteful (supposedly) to the smart world, yet also keep intact his other 'self', the playwright. Thus the promiscuity offered illusions of 'freedom' from a social problem.[19]

Shepherd sees in Orton's personal contradictions the contradictions of many homosexuals in the period leading up to the (partial) decriminalization of consenting male homosexual acts in 1967. Orton was torn between the urge to rebel and the necessity to conform in order to achieve commercial or social success. Orton allied himself closely with fetishized masculinity and a phallic gender in order not to be stereotyped as the effeminate homosexual of popular imagination, and he asked for his stage homo/bisexual characters to be treated likewise.[20] Orton's dislike of effeminacy – he was chided by his lover Halliwell for his insensitivity – was also a tactical alliance with dominant ideas about masculinity, projecting his own powerlessness in relation to his class and position in society on to his powerfulness as sexual predator.

At the same time as he created his public image, Orton was able to create another type of character to send up and spoof polite middle-class sensibilities. He created a fictional character, Edna Welthorpe (Mrs), in a series of public letters between 1958 and 1967. Welthorpe's letters to newspapers, individuals and public companies, berate Orton, the establishment, big firms like Smedley's and Littlewood's in an attempt to confuse and complicate apparently simple viewpoints or criticisms. In Wilde's own terms, the character begs the question of who or what is real, and what is artificial. If Welthorpe (Edna, Mrs) can put across legitimate criticisms of Orton and his work – 'Today's young playwrights take it upon themselves to flaunt their contempt for ordinary decent people',[21] who is the author, who the critic and who the audience? Welthorpe, and the other characters Orton created in his letter-writing campaigns, explore contradictory and conflicting ideas about Orton and his work, and are a means for Orton himself to acknowledge and subvert those very theatrical traditions that he himself felt confined by. I don't wish to overemphasize Welthorpe's importance, but she does show Orton's camp sensibility and represent a prank, an invention, a public intervention in the debate about morality at a time when pressure for law reform around homosexuality and 'moral' issues such as divorce and abortion was very much in the public eye.

In 1951, fears about national security with relation to homosexuality were fuelled by the news that two British spies – Guy Burgess (a homosexual) and Donald MacLean (a bisexual) had in fact been Soviet spies, and defected to Russia. The Labouchère Amendment of 1885, the 'blackmailer's charter', was beginning to come under public scrutiny. In 1954, Peter Wildeblood and Lord Montagu were tried in relation to homosexual offences involving working-class British airmen. The trial aroused such publicity, including questions about the police's invasion of privacy and their questionable 'evidence', that law reform became a necessity – the law had either to be tightened or changed altogether. In April of the same year, a committee (later to become the Wolfenden Committee) was set up to look into the law relating to homosexuality and prostitution (politely referred to in code by some committee members as 'Huntley and Palmer's, makers of a popular biscuit with the same initials as the Committee's sphere of interests).[22] The Wolfenden Report was published on 4 September 1957 and recommended law reform. In May 1958, the Homosexual Law Reform Society – 'a classical middle-class single-issue pressure group'[23] – was set up to lobby for the Report's implementation. Despite its efforts, and although law reform on prostitution was enacted in the Street Offences Act of 1959, it was to be much longer before Wolfenden's proposals were seriously taken up by Parliament.

The 1960s saw homosexuality become more and more public, although not necessarily in a favourable light. The year 1961 saw the release of the films *A Taste of Honey* and *Victim* and Eliot George's novel *The Leather Boys*. Gordon Westwood's *A Minority* (1960) and the Home-Office-sponsored *The Homosexual Society* (1962) provided studies on the subject, and Douglas Plummer's influential book *Queer People* was published the following year. In the theatre, aside from Orton's own plays, there was John Osborne's *A Patriot for Me* and Christopher Hampton's *When Did You Last See My Mother?* (1966) at the Royal Court, despite the Lord Chamberlain's censoring role in English drama until 1968. The press continued to report stories on homosexuality and also covered the ongoing debate about Wolfenden's report in Parliament. In 1963, the *Sunday Mirror* even produced a report on 'How to spot a homo':

> they wear silk shirts and sit up at Chi-Chi bars with full-bosomed ladies. Or they wear hairy sports jackets and give their wives a black eye when they get back from the working men's club. They wrestle, play golf, and work up knots of muscles lifting weights. They are married, have children. They are everywhere, they can be anybody.[24]

The Wolfenden Report was finally implemented in 1967, with the Sexual Offences Act which legalized some homosexual relations between consenting men (over the age of twenty-one) in private. As has been pointed out elsewhere, however, 'These measures did not reflect an acceptance of homosexuality, rather the method and extent of control was refined'.[25] Prosecutions of gay men for many offences radically increased after the law was passed, and the law is still out of step with almost all European legislation.

Joe Orton, the rebel and sexual outlaw, playwright and author, died on 9 August 1967, killed with a series of hammer blows to the head by his lover Kenneth Halliwell, who himself then committed suicide by swallowing twenty-two Nembutals. Like Wilde's trial, Orton's murder has come to prefigure and over-shadow his work and life. Orton the writer, and even Orton the homosexual, have now become Orton The Metaphor. According to Colin Chambers and Mike Prior in the relatively conservative study of post-war British drama, *Playwrights' Progress*, he was 'An *enfant terrible* in the classic Romantic mould . . . Orton revelled in the role of social outcast and was defeated, fatally, by the success with which he played this role out'.[26] Simon Shepherd relates the deaths of Halliwell and Orton 'to the society in which Orton lived, which was (and is) deeply hostile to homosexuality, and through hostility creates misery and deaths of homosexuals'.[27] John Lahr, who edited Orton's diaries for publication, sees in Orton, and in particular the diaries, 'the cock-eyed liberty of the time – a time before the failure of radical politics, before mass unemployment, before AIDS'.[28] The theatre critic Nicholas de Jongh, in turn, sees the deaths of Orton and Halliwell almost as soap opera, 'a domestic tragedy, one of the kind that sometimes befalls heterosexual mar-riages too'.[29]

Orton, once his own creation, has been filtered – re-created – through other narrators of his life-story. The line begins with Kenneth Halliwell, who claims to have started (and influenced) Orton's writing, carries on with Peggy Ramsay, Orton's literary agent, and continues through the discourse between his self-appointed biographer John Lahr and gay critic Simon Shepherd, who villifies Lahr for distortion of Orton (and particularly Halliwell). The mysterious Orton is even re-invented in a film, *Prick Up Your Ears* (based on Lahr's biography) and in plays such as Simon Moss's *Cock-Ups*. His life has itself become a pastiche, which Jonathan Dollimore notes in Orton's defacing of library books and his theories of montage as prefiguring Fredric Jameson's ideal of postmodern pastiche, 'black parody, parody that has lost its humor'.[30] Orton's own writings, his diary, have become a central text for his drama – Lahr admits to using his editorial power so that 'For dramatic symmetry, I have ended the *Diaries* on Orton's and Halliwell's last exchange'.[31] He also claims that 'The diaries are not just a chronicle of the drama between them, but a prop in it',[32] pointing to Halliwell's suicide note as evidence that Orton knew that Halliwell read his 'secret' diaries (the note was found on top of Orton's diaries and read 'If you read his diary all will be explained'). Indeed, the published book's cover shows a pastiche of Orton's body itself, with theatre curtains held back to reveal the top half of a naked Orton, on (in?) which is a clothed, complete picture of Orton. Orton himself is seen to be a 'drama', the visual referring both to farce (the 'revealing' of a nude male) and to subtext (a naked Orton is not necessarily the *real* Orton).

Has Orton, then, been outmanoeuvred by his own creation? In Orton, as in Wilde, we see a continual set of manoeuvres. Creating their own identity, they come into conflict with society, which then tries to redefine them – Wilde as a degenerate and corrupter of youth, Orton as promiscuous and sowing the seeds for his own violent (self)-destruction. At the same time, their works can be assimilated or appropriated, so that Wilde's plays are simply polite comedies of manners, and Orton's works simple bawdy bedroom farces. We have also seen the characters of Wilde and Orton become the focus for another set of tactical manoeuvres, where gay writers and critics attempt to reclaim and re-interpret their lives and works: Bartlett on Wilde in *Who Was Than Man?* and Simon Shepherd on Orton in *Because We're Queers*. It is a pattern we can also see in the life of Rock Hudson, whose carefully constructed straight image was undermined by his HIV infection and subsequent death, an event which left many commentators attributing his closetedness to Hudson's duplicitous sensibility as a homosexual, and not to the homophobia of 1950s America. Richard Meyer, in his analysis of the effects of Hudson's announcement of his illness, quotes theatre critic Frank Rich in *Esquire* magazine:

> Does Hudson's skill at playing a heterosexual mean that he was a brilliant actor, or was this just the way he really was, without acting at all? I suspect that most Americans believed that Hudson, who seemed so natural on screen, was playing

himself, which means that in the summer of 1985 we had to accept the fact that many of our fundamental conventional images of heterosexuality were instilled in us (and not for the first time) by a homosexual . . . everything that happened on screen was a lie, with the real content embedded in code.[33]

The body of a famous – or infamous – homosexual often becomes the site of larger cultural and societal questions (and anxieties) about sexuality, sexual identity and gender. Wilde, Orton and Hudson all represent not just their own creations but the embodiment of a series of historical anxieties around sexuality, and so their meanings, their *role* in society, is constantly being examined and re-examined. The traditional need of modern society to explain homosexuality has led it to the actual body as the place where the answer must be. Perhaps it's in the genes. Perhaps it's to do with hormones or brain cells. Either way, such questions then focus around the identifiable homosexual, both those – like Wilde and Orton – who were always assumed to be a little queer, or those like Rock Hudson who were later discovered to contradict their own public image and social role. Where the body becomes the site for questions around sexual identity, it has to be publicly dissected into its constituent parts so that sexual identity can be categorized, particularly where the social role or importance of an (in)famous public figure brings into question public sensibilities. And if the body can be a battleground around sexuality, it can also be the site for questions around gender, where one of the great complicating (and, for some, disturbing) factors is the theatrical manoeuvre used by gay men for years – cross-dressing.

Notes

1. Herbert Blau, *To All Appearances: Ideology and Performance* (Routledge, 1992), p. 98–9.
2. Richard Meyer, 'Rock Hudson's body', in *Inside/Out: Lesbian Theories, Gay Theories*, ed. Diana Fuss (Routledge, 1991), p. 283.
3. Wayne Kestenbaum, 'The queen's throat: (homo)sexuality and the art of singing', in *Inside/Out*, pp. 209–10.
4. Kestenbaum, 'The queen's throat', p. 207.
5. Dr La Forest Potter, *Strange Loves: A Study in Sexual Abnormalities* (New York: The Robert Dodsley Company, 1933).
6. Michael Bronski, *Culture Clash: The Making of Gay Sensibility* (Boston: Southend Press, 1984), p. 56.
7. Jonathan Dollimore, *Sexual Dissidence* (Oxford: Oxford University Press, 1991), p. 67.
8. Cited in Richard Ellmann, *Oscar Wide* (Harmondsworth: Penguin, 1988), p. 196.
9. Neil Bartlett, *Who Was That Man?* (Serpent's Tail, 1988), p. 163.
10. Bartlett, p. 163.
11. Bartlett, p. 142.
12. Jeffrey Weeks, *Coming Out: Homosexual Politics in Britain* (Quartet Books, 1977), p. 42.
13. Bartlett, p. 181.
14. Bartlett, p. 156.
15. Justice Wills's summing up, cited in Ellmann, *Oscar Wilde*.
16. Dollimore, p. 309.
17. Head of Criminal Investigations Department, Scotland Yard, 1891, cited in Richard Davenport-Hines, *Sex, Death and Punishment* (Fontana Press, 1991), p. 92.
18. Bronski, pp. 57–8.
19. Simon Shepherd, *Because We're Queers: The Life and Crimes of Kenneth Halliwell and Joe Orton* (GMP, 1989), p. 56.
20. Orton, in his notes for an American production of *Loot*, demands that there shouldn't be anything 'queer or camp' about the portrayal of the characters Hal or Dennis – for a full account see John Lahr, *Prick Up Your Ears* (Allen Lane, 1978).
21. 'Edna Welthorpe', letter to the *Daily Telegraph*, in *The Orton Diaries*, ed. John Lahr (Methuen, 1986), p. 283.
22. Davenport-Hines, *Sex, Death and Punishment*, p. 314.
23. Weeks, *Coming Out*, p. 171.
24. Cited in Stephen Jeffrey-Poulter, *Peers, Queers and Commons: The Struggle for Gay Law Reform from 1950 to the Present* (Routledge, 1991), p. 61.
25. Paul Crane, *Gays and the Law* (Pluto Press, 19182), pp. 13–14.

26. Colin Chambers and Mike Prior, *Playwrights' Progress: Patterns of Postwar British Drama* (Amber Lane, 1987), p. 109.
27. Shepherd, *Because We're Queers*, p. 7.
28. Lahr, introduction to *The Orton Diaries*, p. 14.
29. Nicholas de Jongh, *Not in Front of the Audience: Homosexuality on Stage* (Routledge, 1992), p. 105.
30. Cited in Dollimore, *Sexual Dissidence*, p. 315.
31. Lahr, editor's note, *The Orton Diaries*, p. 9.
32. Lahr, introduction to *The Orton Diaries*, p. 21.
33. Frank Rich, 'The gay decades', *Esquire* (November 1987), cited in Meyer, 'Rock Hudson's body', p. 278.

Chapter two

A Pair of Stillies and a Little Bit of Lippy

Arnold: See, I'm among the last of a dying breed. Once the ERA and gay civil rights bills have been passed, me and mine will find ourselves swept under the carpets like the blacks done to Amos, Andy and Aunt Jemima. But that's all right too. With a voice and face like this I got nothing to worry about, I can always drive a cab. And that, chillun, is called power. Be it gay, black, or flowered, it always comes down to the survival of the majority.

. . . There are easier things in this life than being a drag queen. But I ain't got no choice. Try as I may, I just can't walk in flats.

Harvey Fierstein, The International Stud[1]

THE trial of two cross-dressers known as Fanny and Stella in 1870 demonstrated the potential for both success and failure in cross-dressing as a theatrical manoeuvre. Boulton and Park (Fanny and Stella's street drag aliases) had successfully passed for women for many years before being arrested on 28 April 1870. Yet their very arrest and the court trial afterwards were subverted because of the fact that in order to prosecute the two transgressors successfully, the judiciary would have to acknowledge what Boulton and Park were – male sodomites – and thereby deny the failure of the dominant gender system in interpreting, encoding and *defining* sexual and gender identity. Fanny and Stella do not by any means mark the beginning of a tradition linking queers with cross-dressing, but they do represent one of our successes and, paradoxically, one of our failures. The contradictions in the case against them – making them visible as men dressed as women, as Neil Bartlett has lovingingly pointed out in his 'Present for Mr Oscar Wilde', *Who Was That Man?* – show that Fanny and Stella were themselves made invisible, unreal, asexual; the proof of their own bodies as sexual was denied them. Although they were charged with conspiracy to commit a felony, it was successfully argued that by drawing so much attention to themselves, the two men could not possibly have been intent on committing such a scandalous act as sodomy – a disgrace one would want to keep most private. It is in these circumstances that it is useful to look at the case around Fanny and Stella in a wider sense in order to understand the scope and possibilities for acknowledging the body as a more confusing signifier of gender than many would like to believe.

Although drag is closely associated with modern gay identity and gay (sub)culture, cross-dressing as a term covers many more patterns of cross- or trans-gender behaviour and actions. Cross-dressing can cover male and female, homosexual and heterosexual, transsexual, transvestite and drag behaviour and can be sexual or non-sexual, depending on intent, content and context. Cross-dressing behaviour occurs cross- and trans-culturally, in ancient and modern, urban and rural communities. Different forms and meaning of cross-dressing can be attached, for example, to shamanic behaviour during the Old Stone Age, the Native American *berdaches*, Joan of Arc, the *travesti* of post-war Europe, the jazz musician Billy Tipton and the rad-fems of the Gay Liberation Front. Although there may be similarities in some or all of these cultures, readings of the effects and meanings of cross-dressing vary from period to period and from society to society. However, it would be fair to say that western gay identities – particularly the arrival of *queerness* – have a close affinity with gender-bending behaviour and dress, and that this has a peculiar tradition within Britain. And this is as much to do with the way society is structured as with what is worn and where.

In *Vested Interests: Cross-Dressing & Cultural Anxiety,*

Marjorie Garber has written that 'No analysis of "cross-dressing" that wants to interrogate the phenomenon seriously from a cultural, political, or even aesthetic vantage point can fail to take into account the foundational role of gay identity and gay style'.[2] She goes on to assert that '*transvestism is a space of possibility structuring and confounding culture*: the disruptive element that intervenes, not just a category crisis of male and female, but the crisis of category itself' (Garber's emphasis).[3] The presentation of gender identity or allegiance becomes a point of contest, throwing into confusion binary categories so that the event itself becomes the crisis of binarism, challenging the accepted oppositional nature of gender. It can be seen, and has been used, as a theatrical manoeuvre. In particular, gay male cross-dressing is self-consciously so. As the gay writer Kris Kirk pointed out in *Men in Frocks*. 'A man can only put on a skirt self-consciously; however he does it, it always seems like a gesture'.[4] The street queens are not only the inheritants of a long legacy but also the creators of opportunity, consciously exploring the 'space of possibility' to complicate that most ambiguous of terrains – the body itself.

　　Although much attention to male cross-dressing has focused on the Renaissance period, and especially on the theatrical use of it on stage, Judy Grahn has explored the specifically gay use of cross-dressing in a much more ambitious and ambiguous manner, tracing it back to the Middle Ages in Europe. Grahn's alternative gay history, *Another Mother Tongue*, is a fascinating search for queer culture through the ages. Her speculations on the origin of drag queens are particularly of interest and, in the context of theatricality and ritual, pertinent. She sees the role of the modern drag queen as 'like the king's jester without the king, some theatrical combination of the Fool, the Hanged Man, and the Empress all rolled into one and without a true territory'.[5] Her analogies are not chosen without reason. Grahn sees the very word 'drag' as a throwback to slang for 'coach' or 'cart', used in early European festivities: 'In its most historic sense, being "in drag" is a reference to cross-dressing during New Year's processions when the Fool's King, a female queen god, or the goat-king Puck was pulled in a cart'.[6] Although Grahn's ideas are mostly speculative, the idea of Middle Age drag queens as the centre of festivities and celebrations is an appealing one, and one she directly relates to the American Hallowe'en parades, major festivals in the 'gay calendar'.

In Britain, cross-dressing was traditionally banned by the Puritans, who quoted the authority of the Book of Deuteronomy: 'The woman shall not wear that which pertaineth unto a man, neither shall a man put on a woman's garment; for all that do so are an abomination unto the Lord thy God' (Deut. 22: 5). The 1620 pamphlets *Hic Mulier: or, The Man-Woman* and *Haec Vir: or, The Womanish-Man* represented concern and debate not only over breaking the rule of Deuteronomy and the problems of cross-dressing, but the effects of cross-dressing on the ordering of gender and class. According to Jonathan Dollimore, the producers of these pamphlets

> feared that 'doing' what a woman does (on the stage, and in women's clothes) leads to 'being' what a woman is; the most unmanageable anxiety is that there is no essentially masculine self, and cross-dressing in women's clothes can lead to a man 'turning into' a woman.[7]

The use of boy actors on stage to play 'women's' parts thus brought into question not only the rule of Deuteronomy but the question of identity itself. Marjorie Garber also acknowledges this potential crisis:

> Renaissance anti-theatricalists, in their debates about gender, cross-dressing and the stage, articulated deep-seated anxieties about the possibility that identity was not fixed, that there was no underlying 'self' at all, and that therefore identities had to be zealously and jealously safeguarded.[8]

Garber goes on to conclude that 'actors were in effect *allowed* to violate the sumptuary laws that governed dress as social station – on the supposedly "safe" space of the stage'. Which also becomes 'a privileged site of transgression',[9] where actors could violate normal dress-rules regarding class and gender. Safely on stage, the boy actors could be seen as diffusing the questions of gender and identity because they were themselves defined by the space they were

performing in; they were performing for, and controlled by, normative social and gender structures as represented in their audiences.
They were on stage, and the performances ended after the productions, even if the theatre had by then attracted a lubricious reputation for itself. However, theatrical representations on stage were
beginning to become more and more related to sexual behaviour –
and particularly sexual *identities* – off stage by the end of the
seventeenth century.

The bisexual libertine, the rake, as he appeared on the Res-
toration stage of the 1660s and 1670s was not associated necessarily with a distinct homosexual behaviour, but rather seen as
transgressive in many philosophical and social respects, with sexual
behaviour but one symptom. The dawning of the eighteenth century, however, saw a recategorization of identities, and changing
patterns of behaviour introduced firstly the effeminate fop, whose
behaviour mirrored much of the rake's narcissism but was rarely
connected with (homo)sexual activity. But, as Randolph Trumbach
has pointed out, there was another and more far-reaching change
taking place, which had a direct effect on the association of cross-
dressing with (homo)sexual identity: the rise of the 'molly'.

> After 1720 the fop's effeminacy, in real life and on the stage,
> came to be identified with the effeminacy of the then emerg-
> ing role of the exclusive adult sodomite – known in the
> ordinary language of his day as a *molly*, and later as a
> *queen*.[10]

The rise of the cross-dressing molly in Britain, associated with
same-sex behaviour (although he was often married), accompanies
such developments in Europe. During the seventeenth century,
there are accounts of transvestite balls in the Dutch Republic, and
records of transvestism in Naples and Sicily. The molly frequented
the descendant of the seventeenth-century homosexual brothel, or –
as it became known – the molly house, which became both meeting
place and subculture.

There were many molly houses in London during the early
eighteenth century, one of the most famous being Margaret Clap's
house in Field Lane, Holborn. The molly houses were frequently

taverns, but always secret meeting places for effeminate homosexuals and their partners to meet and act out their own homosexual rituals (to be discussed more fully in chapter 7). The customers at the molly houses frequently cross-dressed as women, and gave each other women's names, acting out an excessively effeminate role, often in contrast to the roles they played outside the molly house itself. The queens who frequented molly houses rarely wore their clothes outside or in the street – the molly house was a secret(ish) place, despite the constant threats of raids by the police. One description of the molly houses gives a full account of their type of dress:

> Some were completely rigged in gowns, petticoats, head-cloths, fine laced shoes, furbelowed scarves, and masks; some had riding hoods; some were dressed like milkmaids, others like shepherdesses with green hats, waistcoats, and petticoats; and others had their faces patched and painted and wore very expensive hoop petticoats, which had been very lately introduced.[11]

The molly houses, although secret, were well enough known about to have been easily located. They were characterized by and became known for their radical gender inversions. Alan Bray, in *Homosexuality in Renaissance England*, acknowledges their importance in this very role. In a reading which could be interpreted as signifying camp, drag both defined and created their existence: 'the one element in them that most scandalised contemporary journalists writing about the molly house was the extravagant effeminacy and transvestism they could involve; and this was at the root of the way they worked'.[12] Bray notes that what was also remarkable about molly house transvestism was that it was not designed to deceive but was a statement itself. Much cross-dressing (male and female) was designed so that the wearer could pass as a member of the opposite sex. For many women (legendarily as pirates or soldiers), this may have been one of the few routes to power or success. The mollies, however, created identities for themselves which were self-consciously playing with gender roles and, at the same time as giving the appearance of effeminacy, acknowledging the all-male atmosphere and company. Transvestism in the molly houses was a theatrical manoeuvre which accompanied rituals and ceremonies creating and affirming a (homo)sexual subculture, centred on and creating opportunities for same-sex behaviour. Their unique existence is largely due to the gay nature of these 'private' clubs and their inhabitants – 'Effeminacy and transvestism with specifically homosexual connotations were a crucial part of what gave the molly houses their identity'.[13]

The (perhaps unlikely) inheritors of the molly houses are the street queens and drag queens of today, the rad-fems and gender-benders of modern Britain. Their particular sets of histories can be traced back to just after the Second World War, and are themselves part of a theatrical tradition. While the *travesti* were becoming popular and successful in continental Europe, the chorus queens were touring Britain and entertaining the armed forces abroad. The original shows, where servicemen cross-dressed as women and entertained their peers, became supplanted as many non-servicemen saw in the shows and their companies a route which might protect and feed their own sexual identities. Kris Kirk, in *Men in Frocks*, realized the importance of post-war revues such as *Soldiers in Skirts*, *Misleading Ladies* and *Showboat Express*, 'but their importance has been marginalised because they helped change the world by stealth'.[14] Queers found in the shows not only validation of their own sexuality and culture but also economic and physical survival, as well as trade:

> When we went to Portsmouth the theatre was packed with sailors, hundreds of matelots. Looking out from the stage you could see all these white hats in the gallery. And when we came out of the stage door, they filled the streets. The police had to remove them from the stage door; you would have thought royalty was arriving.[15]

The performing troops/troupes were not always made welcome by their hosts, and Kirk's account of the fabulous 1940s queens is punctuated by accounts of society's reactions to their outlandishness and daring. Rigid gender roles were expected and imposed, so that even minor deviations from the traditional suit and short back and sides were frowned upon and caused immediate reactions. Ironically, the drag that brought the performers success and acceptance on stage also isolated them socially off stage, creating and necessitating a community where security depended on a strong bond of loyalty within the group. The affinity with sailors and troops continued as more and more drag queens joined the navy, or gathered around seaports. These queens often became the focus for attention not only during shows but at parties and frequently received unsolicited interest from the police:

> One day Stella [Stella Minge, a drag queen renowned in the 1960s for her parties] went down to the local police station because she was going to be away from her house for a while and she didn't like the idea of it standing empty. 'Constable, I'd like you to keep an eye on my house,' she said. 'Stella,' he replied, 'we've been keeping an eye on your house for donkeys' years.'[16]

Many of the modern drag queens had their origins on board the ships, and for some it was a natural transition when gay pubs began welcoming drag acts during the 1960s and 1970s. The period was also witness to a change in attitudes, so that the rise of feminism saw gender and its construction in dress as a suitable target for criticism and reform. While women challenged the bra by burning it and took up unisex fashion, the hippy counter-culture flirted with clothing as statement, and in particular men's clothing became more flamboyant and colourful. For the famous, it became fashionable to play with gender roles, and act out complicating and contradictory identities, a process led by David Bowie and Mick Jagger, and continued through the 1980s and 1990s by the New Romantics and gender-bending antics of Boy George. Such developments have not been without their fair share of (often justified) criticism. Michael Bronski sees rock music's assimilation of drag/androgyny as a theatrical manoeuvre to be fraudulently liberal – both manipulative and consumerist:

> In the rock world, entertainers are inseparable from advertising. The Rollings Stones' and Boy George's images *are*

their ads. Because sex is the foundation of much advertising philosophy, and because gay men are often connected with sex, many gay images have found their way into popular culture as techniques to sell things.[17]

However, at the same time there also arose a political consciousness which used drag as a technique and critique of heteosexism and homophobia, beginning with those drag queens who helped to sow the seeds of Gay Liberation itself at the Stonewall riots in 1969. The emerging Gay Liberation Front of the early 1970s in Britain saw an influx of drag queens, 'rad-fems', who consciously chose to rebel against repressive gender dressing and definitions by wearing drag or androgynous clothing. They would challenge the assumptions of 'the men' and act out subversive gestures during meetings – knitting and gossiping in the front row if there was too much macho posturing or posing. Bette Bourne, now a member of the theatre group Bloolips, described his first appearance in drag at a GLF conference and its effect on him:

> When I got into drag I felt totally transformed. When I think about it, it brings tears to my eyes. I felt sensuous and relaxed in an extraordinary way. I sat down at the meeting. I don't know much about politics – I hadn't read many books and I hadn't been to college – but there was one particular college boy stomping around and giving it all out, not letting anyone else get a word in. This time, I started talking – and he listened. I sat with a cigarette, just sending him up. What I was wearing so overwhelmed him that was then that I realised the power of a man wearing drag, as opposed to impersonating a woman – which is something I've never done.[18]

The drag queens in GLF were often involved in the street theatre group, using elaborate theatrical manoeuvres to 'zap' homophobic events and personalities such as the Miss World contest and the fundamentalist and anti-gay Festival of Light. The 'zaps' often incorporated drag into the action, and the rad-fems in the GLF used drag as costume in their everyday lives, often living communally and outraging local communities with their gender reversals. The rad-fems made strong links with the women's movement, and at their strongest influenced not only other drag queens but also the politicos and 'machos' in the GLF itself. Aubrey Walter, in his Introduction to *Come Together – The Years of Gay Liberation 1970–73*, describes a lecturer who had been married, and had a kid, who got into drag because of:

> a guilt feeling about being male and having been straight, oppressing his wife and acting like a real 'man'. He would travel around wearing rather bizarre clothes, like a short sort of crimplene shift frock, rather run-down sling-backs, wild long thin hair, fairly conventional make-up and a hand-bag. Whenever he went on public transport he would be mocked and laughed at by people, and threatened and thrown off buses. So he developed this really aggressive manner of getting on tubes and buses, glaring round and threatening the other passengers first – he would also deliver his lectures in drag. Everyone thought he was really brave.[19]

Walter notes that it was the drag queens – traditionally frowned upon by assimilationist homosexual rights campaigners – who were taking the lead in the GLF and discovering a voice for themselves, one which had been often denied to them by a gay community more intent on proving itself as responsible, respectable and deserving liberal tolerance and equality. Yet, historically, it is the drag queens and cross-dressers who have been at the very centre of debates around sexuality and sexual identity, and who have provided the most daring challenges to conformity and normative practices. Although GLF and the rad-fems declined as quickly as they had risen, the theatrical manoeuvre they learnt led many into theatre – where, for example, Bette Bourne and Bloolips continue success-fully to combine politics with entertainment – or into continuing to fight for gay rights in the press, publishing, business, media or the international gay movement. Moreover, the GLF and rad-fems paved the way in Britain for campaigns such as the Stop the Clause movement in 1988, and groups such as OutRage! and the Sisters of Perpetual Indulgence.

The Sisters of Perpetual Indulgence are an order of gay male nuns, whose professed mission is the expiation of stigmatic guilt and the promulgation of universal joy. They originated in America – beginning as an order at the appropriate time of Easter 1979 – but the current British house was set up as a mission from Sydney in 1990. Their use of traditional nuns' habits – veil, wimple and all – is concerned not with religiosity but with *public manifestation* – the very fact of gay visibility. The habit is self-consciously worn to publicize the nun's sexuality, rather than to hide or veil it. The Sisters also have a peculiar (if not a trifle queer) legacy. If cross-dressing has been a frequent theatrical manoeuvre for gay men, male nuns have a particular history to themselves. Garber notes that 'The male nun, the female monk, the feminized Jewish man are recurrent figures of fantasy as well as of history and propaganda'.[20] She also records that during the eighteenth century, 'ecclesiastical dress was a favorite kind of travesty, charged with erotic significance', citing men dressed in nun's habits as one source of parody of the Catholic church's extravagant use of costume and finery.[21] The sight of a man in a nun's habit in Charlotte Brontë's *Villette*, according to scholar Joseph Litvak in a radical re-reading of the novel, can be seen 'less as an emblem of plenitude and interiority than as a floating signifier, a ghostly harbinger of *différance*'.[22] Kaeir Curtin records that after the close of Mae West's infamous and controversial 1927 play *The Drag*, an anonymous newspaper articled claimed that:

> Another celebrated homo said to have played in *The Drag* is called 'Mother Superior.' This character is an indefatigable correspondent. He is said to have studied for the priesthood at one time, but abandoned taking holy orders for the more exciting life of a homosexual in the great city. 'Mother Superior' is the confessor and spiritual advisor of a large group of homos and both he and 'The Duchess' hold court in a certain eating place on Fifth Avenue in the forties. Whenever a publication takes the queer clan to task, it is always 'Mother Superior' or 'The Duchess' who wrote a defense…[23]

The GLF zap on the Festival of Light – and other demonstrations – involved nuns (as we shall see later). In 1983, after being arrested on an anti-nuclear demonstration, the gay writer Robert Glück records that on Gay Freedom Day in the Santa Rita County jail one group of prisoners turned 'sheets and blankets into wimples and habits: Sisters of Perpetual Incarceration'.[24] Boy George used to dress as a nun, and films as diverse as *The Magic Christian*, *Bedazzled* and *Nuns on the Run* show representations of, and an interest in, male nuns. Marjorie Garber quotes Sister Boom Boom, one of the American Sisters of Perpetual Indulgence, in her analysis of the phenomenon:

> 'Nun of the above' – Sister Boom Boom's flippant political slogan – in fact describes quite well the psychogenesis of this haunting figure of the transvestite nun. The third space – the space of thirdness – is simultaneously demarcated, filled, and emptied out by the phantom nun – the nun (or 'none') that calls into question categories of male and female, Catholic and Protestant, English and French, gay and straight: in Wallace Steven's words, 'nothing that is not there, and the nothing that is.'[25]

The Sisters might be seen as queer – undefined and outside of definition – in the most literal sense, taking on the role of the cross-dressing shaman rather than the moralistic fundamentalist. The habit is designed to confuse, complicate and create possibilities of change and transformation. The promulgation of universal joy therefore becomes a collective and personal mission, acting as 'an antidote to the oppressive effects of gender role and behaviour forced upon women and men in our society'.[26] The clothes themselves attract attention, but also invite debate and contradiction. The purpose of the habit – public manifestation – is a theatrical manoeuvre used to assert gay men's presence, wherever and whenever the Sisters deem fit – this might be on Gay Pride marches, anti-war marches, in discos (gay or straight), as fundraisers for HIV charities, in football matches or on motorbikes. When Benetton used a picture of an AIDS activist dying in the arms of his family for an advertising campaign in 1992, the presence of the Sisters on ACT-UP demos in Benetton shops, displacing displays and 'trashing' the store, attracted much attention in the press precisely because of the nuns' own clothes and manner of dress – a fashion display with politics. In addition, the habit itself (usually entirely covering the body, although many 'variations' have sought to reveal it) has been associated with protection. This may be collective, for the gay community as a whole: 'We do all the work that catholic nuns have done for centuries. We are 21st century nuns'.[27] Alternatively, it may be on an individual, and more literal, level. Although the habit attracts attention, the Sisters have often commented that it also protects against unnecessary (or violent) reactions: 'lesbians and gays are hassled every day – in some ways, wearing a habit affords us some protection because we are so visible. Nobody wants to be seen beating up a nun'.[28] The Sisters marry form and content, so that the 'mission' of the Order (the group, or body, of nuns) is incomplete without the habit – 'We are artists as well as social activists and our faces and our bodies are our canvases'.[29]

The challenge that cross-dressing poses is not simply one of costume. Marjorie Garber asserts that the wearer is an emblem of crisis itself, that in the category of the cross-dresser we see society's own confusions and contradictions. Importantly, cross-dressing itself has different meanings depending on when, where and how it is appropriated as a tactic, manoeuvre or costume. As Carole Anne Taylor points out in an essay on drag and cross-dressing, 'It is important to read each instance of drag (and its interpretations) symptomatically rather than to insist it is always radical or conservative'.[30] If, as the Sisters of Perpetual Indulgence claim, the body is a canvas, a neutral space, then cross-dressing is a dressing of the set, not simply an inversion of what is already there (this being much more of a conservative theatrical manoeuvre which, I would suggest, is behind much 'straight' drag, for example that of comedian Benny Hill). What cross-dressing implies, then, is that gender (male/female identity) is not necessarily written on to the body but is a system of codes and beliefs held by the readers of the body, that gender is socially constructed. The claim of male to female transsexuals that they are actually women in men's bodies is a literal translation of the encoding system of gender. This interpretation of cross-dressing is by no means accepted by all theorists, but in the context of theatrical manoeuvres, it does open up a spectrum of possibilities which goes beyond 'putting on a frock'. Wearing a frock in the theatre, 'passing' as a woman in the street, and being visibly recognized as a cross-dressing man in the street, are all very different scenarios, with different (but not necessarily foreseeable) effects.

Further, cross-dressers are re-appropriating their own bodies, not just to perform but as the space on which performance takes place. By locating the performance as self, the cross-dresser becomes a protagonist. When Quentin Crisp walked down the road during the 1930s and 1940s with make-up and outrageous clothes, he was aware of being 'queer', of being watched, of being a 'spectacle'. The danger here is that this is the only view, that the 'exotic' becomes marginalized or ghettoized rather than radical and/or threatening. Cross-dressers can be seen as the 'Trojan horses' of queer theatrical manoeuvres – a gender bomb which can be detonated at any time. Modern groups such as the Sisters and OutRage! have been able to use this device – on the London Underground, at church services and political meetings – both to disguise (homo)sexual presence, and then to reveal and publicize it. There's nothing like a dame when the cameras are out.

The link with the molly houses and characters like Fanny and Stella can perhaps encourage us to see a heritage in the cross-dressers, to value rather than ridicule them. Assimilationists still see cross-dressing and overt effeminacy as an embarrassment, but there are certainly grounds to say that Fanny and Stella had more in common with the 1969 Stonewall riots and the birth of a 'gay consciousness' than the Homosexual Law Reform Society did. Cross-dressing is not only one of the emblems of gay culture, it is part of it. Whereas during the 1950s and 1960s many gay men might have claimed that the only difference between them and straights was what they did in bed, in the AIDS crisis we might claim this as the only similarity. Difference and diversity, essential parts of the queer agenda, can be seen at their most complicated, colourful and potentially efficacious, in the role of cross-dressing as a theatrical manoeuvre. Perhaps the last word on cross-dressing in all its complex theatricality should (as ever) be left to the inimitable Bette Bourne:

> We kick over the stereotypes . . . there's a gag in one of the shows where someone says something about my impersonating Hedy Lamarr. 'Oh,' I say. 'I thought I was imitating John Gielgud imitating Hedy Lamarr.'[31]

Notes

1. Harvey Fierstein, *The International Stud*, in *Torch Song Trilogy*, (Methuen, 1984), scene 1, p. 6.
2. Marjorie Garber, introduction to *Vested Interests: Cross-Dressing & Cultural Anxiety* (Routledge, 1992), p. 4.
3. Garber, introduction to *Vested Interests*, p. 17.
4. Kris Kirk and Ed Heath, *Men in Frocks* (GMP, 1984), p. 9.
5. Judy Grahn, *Another Mother Tongue: Gay Words, Gay Worlds* (Boston: Beacon Press, 1984), p. 87.
6. Grahn, *Another Mother Tongue*, pp. 95–6.
7. Jonathan Dollimore, *Sexual Dissidence*, (Oxford: Oxford University Press, 1991), p. 252.
8. Garber, *Vested Interests*, p. 32.
9. Garber, *Vested Interests*, p. 40.
10. Randolph Trumbach, 'The birth of the queen: sodomy and the emergence of gender equality in modern culture, 1660–1750', in *Hidden From History: Reclaiming the Gay & Lesbian Past*, ed. Martin Bauml Duberman, Martha Vicinus and George Chauncey Jnr (New York, New American Library, 1989), p. 252.
11. *Select Trials*, vol. 2, pp. 257–8, cited in Alan Bray, *Homosexuality in Renaissance England* (GMP, 1982), p. 87.
12. Bray, p. 86.
13. Bray, p. 88.
14. Kirk and Heath, *Men in Frocks*, p. 15.
15. Poppy Cooper, recorded in Kirk and Heath, *Men in Frocks*, p. 24.
16. Bluebell, quoted in *Men in Frocks*, p. 32.
17. Michael Bronski, *Culture Clash* (Boston: Southend Press, 1984), p. 185.
18. Bette Bourne, in *Men in Frocks*, p. 102.
19. Aubrey Walter, introduction to *Come Together – The Years of Gay Liberation 1970–73*, (GMP, 1980), p. 23.
20. Garber, *Vested Interests*, p. 213.
21. Garber, p. 219.
22. Joseph Litvak, *Caught in the Act: Theatricality in the Nineteenth-*

Century English Novel (Berkeley: University of California Press, 1992), p. 105.

23. Untitled New York newspaper article, 11 December 1927, cited in Kaier Curtin, *We Can Always Call Them Bulgarians* (Boston: Alyson Publications Inc., 1987), p. 98.

24. Robert Glück, 'A little prison journal', in *Heterosexuality*, ed. Gillian E. Hanscombe and Martin Humphries (GMP, 1987), p. 120.

25. Garber, *Vested Interests*, p. 223.

26. Order of Perpetual Indulgence, 'Green tract', 1990.

27. Sisters of Perpetual Indulgence San Francisco, *Rules of Order*, 1992. p. 6.

28. '20 things you always wanted to know about the Sisters of Perpetual Indulgence', London Order of Perpetual Indulgence, 1992.

29. Sisters of Perpetual Indulgence San Francisco, *Rules of Order*, 1992, p. 5.

30. Carole Anne Taylor, 'Boys will be girls: the politics of gay drag', in *Inside/Outside*, ed. Diana Fuss (Routledge, 1991), p. 33.

31. Kirk and Heath, *Men in Frocks*, p. 102.

Chapter three

Anti Bodies

J. R.: A friend was telling me yesterday: when he beats off?
He fantasises it's four or five years ago, before . . . He can't
even fantasise *he's doing what he wants to do with another*
man unless it's before . . . all this.

Robert Chesley, Jerker or The Helping Hand[1]

SINCE 1981, AIDS (Acquired Immune Deficiency Syndrome) and HIV (Human Immuno-Deficiency Virus) have had a
profound effect on gay lifestyles, identities and representation. For
over a decade, our relationships have been formed around and
informed by the impact of HIV on friends, lovers, family, communities. First and most severely in Britain by what has become known
as 'the AIDS crisis', the gay community has loved and lost, cried,
shouted and protested its rights and its grief to a world that still
hasn't comprehended the significance of HIV and AIDS, and still
hasn't adapted in the way that most gay men have had to. In AIDS
campaigns, we are frequently urged to act out our desires, and act
out a range of sexual choices, which are safe, or safer than those
'fashionable' (for want of a better word) a decade ago. That decade
of organizing, protesting, caring and learning has given us groups,
ideas and support networks such as the Terrence Higgins Trust, the
London Lighthouse, the National AIDS Trust, ACT-UP (the AIDS
Coalition to Unleash Power), GMFA (Gay Men Fighting AIDS) and
many more organisations, helplines, charities and information networks.

We've been given theatre and theatre groups, all centred on AIDS – Positive Underground Theatre Company, Common Body, *The Normal Heart*, *Angels in America*, *As Is*, *Compromised Immunity*, dozens of Theatre-in-Education projects and many personal dramatized testimonies in theatre, radio and television. There's even been talk of 'AIDS drama' or – more significantly – 'AIDS theatre'. If AIDS is, as we've been told, and as we continue to see, one of the biggest challenges the modern world has had to face in the twentieth century, then it is only right that theatre, and the arts in general, should reflect, debate, dramatize, attempt to make sense of, these developments and concerns. Theatre, the most public of the arts, the art form which most encourages participation, debate, involvement, a sense of communal presence, is the most obvious – and most useful – art form to tackle such a major issue.

Yet this is not the case. British theatre, whose performers, directors, writers, technicians and critics have been so affected by AIDS and HIV, has made a very poor response to the subject and challenge of AIDS. Mainstream theatre has largely ignored the 'problem', heterosexualized the context in order to make it more 'universal' (commercial), or allowed us the honour of viewing imported (mainly American) plays, most of which have already been proved, that is achieved major success, in America. The West End remains terrified by the *reality* of HIV and AIDS, while at the same time donating huge amounts of time and energy to raising money for AIDS-related charities via gala benefits. Although this is admirable work, the politics of charity work around a major national health crisis and (lack of) government responsibility remain blissfully in the wings while the show, and the band, play on. At a conference on HIV and theatre at the Riverside Studios in 1991, the only significant attendance was by young people's theatre companies, or Theatre-in-Education companies. None of the major theatres was represented, or (apparently) interested. So AIDS becomes the terrain of young people's, or educational, theatre. The latter does some very good work, but also lifts the responsibility of tackling difficult issues from school governors, teachers, local and centralized authorities. With so many subjects on the National Curriculum, so much pressure on teachers to complete assessments and reports, and on schools to opt out of local authority control, what school wouldn't welcome input on HIV/AIDS from an outside agency?

As the National AIDS Trust's Youth Initiative shows, inter-active drama is a useful tool in HIV education and in exploring broader issues around the subject.[2] HIV drama workshops, Drama-in-Education and Theatre-in-Education are all useful tools – the-atrical manoeuvres aimed to raise awareness – and have a very useful part to play in preventative action. This theatrical manoeuvre has in fact been used by pupils themselves – in one Kent grammar school, sixth form pupils tutor their peers on issues around HIV, with activities using dance, art, music and drama. As a result, the school has also been instrumental in touring a safe sex play and cabaret around local schools and youth clubs[3]. In this context, drama becomes a form for empowerment, not inaction. Moreover, drama workshops are generally carefully structured, providing a safe space in which to explore fears and concerns. In this way, role-playing and drama 'games' can help protagonists to 'rehearse' events, plan strategies, examine possible consequences. While it would be naive to assume that this form of drama can provide answers to everyone's problems, or challenges, it would be true to say that such exercises can increase confidence and aware-ness and are valuable to this extent.

The earliest plays to deal with HIV or AIDS were largely produced by and for the gay community, as a means to cope with and react against the unknown. The two earliest plays – *Anti Body* by Louise Kelley in 1983 and *Compromised Immunity* by Andy Kirby in 1985 – both strongly reflect contemporary events and concerns being reported at the time, and warnings that the 'gay plague' (*sic*) was likely to affect a significant number of hetero-sexuals as well as homosexuals. Both plays also emphasized the importance of action and change – particularly changing behav-iour, lifestyle and attitudes. Since there was very little accurate or non-judgemental information around at the time of the plays the productions themselves became part of an information network, bringing people together to watch, discuss and become informed about a relatively new syndrome. Both plays were produced before Section 28 was enforced, but also reflect the homophobia and fear which helped to create the climate for such legislation to be passed – and, in the case of Gay Sweatshop (who toured *Compromised Immunity*) to focus support within the arts and gay communities against such attacks.

Although the plays are two years apart, they are very similar both in structure (relatively simple narratives) and subject matter (AIDS patients coming to terms with their illnesses and lives, and tackling the prejudices or inaction of those around them). Although now dated, and recognizably early 'AIDS dramas', both plays nevertheless deserve greater investigation and recognition.

Anti Body was produced by Consenting Adults In Public at the Cockpit Theatre, London, in 1983. The year before, the Terrence Higgins Trust had been set up, named after one of the first British people to die as a result of AIDS-related illness and dedicated to providing information and practical help on all AIDS matters. In 1983, the number of AIDS cases in Britain was fifteen. The disease was seen primarily as an American problem, and in particular the problem of gay men in America. Orignally called GRID (Gay Related Immune Deficiency), the syndrome had been ascribed to gay lifestyles – promiscuity and drugs, notably poppers or amyl nitrate.

Anti Body itself, given its data and the information available, is a reassuringly well-balanced play, tackling the results of one person's diagnosis as having AIDS. At the beginning of the play, William Davis (a thirty-year-old gay man) is in a hospital in Cambridge with disturbing symptoms – loss of weight, sweats and chills, and intestinal problems. A friend, David, visits him in the hospital and suggests the name of a gay doctor, Arthur Helbing, who might be able to take a look at William and diagnose what is wrong with him. The following scene establishes Helbing's diagnosis – AIDS. William's protestations that it couldn't be, as he was monogamous until he broke up with a long-term lover, Dan, a few months ago, is punctuated by assertions of William's faith in the two men he did have sex with in New York. His reactions to Dr Helbing's questions concerning the two men epitomize many of the views of 'otherness' around AIDS at the time:

they told me they'd never really had an open relationship but they both found me attractive and since I was a visitor I couldn't threaten their relationship, so they agreed that just this once they'd try a threesome. Don't you see? They trusted me, I was special. They made an exception just for me, that's what they said.[4]

William's symptoms are described and explained, not only for the benefit of the patient but also for the audience. AIDS, he is told, is not necessarily fatal – but very little is known about the way it works, or what in fact causes it. A series of visitors – his mother Elisabeth, brother Steve and sister Vanessa, lesbian activists Becky and Jeannie and gay friends John and Malcolm – all help to show different responses to William's news while placing him strongly within a family and social context. Their reactions are explored as much as William's own response to his illness, all shrouded in unknown quantities. The personal and political collide when David asks William if he'd attend a Lesbian and Gay Switchboard symposium on AIDS, along with his doctor. Helbing, professionally, realizes that such an event might be useful, even if it means risking his own discreet sexual identity in being associated so closely with a 'gay disease'. For William, however, such a challenge proves far too difficult personally and leads to a sharp exchange with his friend David, who replies to William's suggestion that he is being used as an exhibit and would be there for publicity value only by guilt-tripping William about his responsibilities:

If a great many come, it won't be because of you, or Dr. Helbing or me or anyone. They'll come to it because they're starting to be frightened, as well they should be. I asked you only because as an activist I thought you still cared about your Gay brothers. But I guess I was wrong! (Act One, scene 6)

The first act closes with a reunion between William and his former lover Dan. Honestly re-appraising their relationship, the scene ends with William refusing sexual contact with Dan on the grounds that he might infect him with AIDS – 'I love you too much to make love, as it were'.

The second act opens with William now moved to a room in a London hospital two months later, having deteriorated in health and feeling much more vulnerable and frustrated. He and his mother argue over their reactions to his deteriorating health, while Dr Helbing illustrates both his own frustration with and faith in the medical research being carried out – hope in the United States, he points out, is on a new drug, Isoprinosine. Presented with a certificate from the Lesbian and Gay Switchboard he had spent time working for, William begins to realize that somehow things have to go on, to move forward. His suggestion that his friends go out and have a few drinks, even pick up, is met with resistance. Not only do they find it difficult to deal with his frankness, but the suggestion that gay men should carry on having sex in the middle of an epidemic brings sharp criticism from his sister, Vanessa:

> You just have to be the biggest fool ever – you're the one lying here with your whole system poisoned because you were out screwing all over the place like a mink on heat. And you're the one that just told your friends here to go out and pick up somebody – hey, maybe they won't be as lucky as you. Maybe they'll have to settle for herpes or syphilis or a simple case of crabs. Why not? After all, it's vital for a stud to get some, all the time, or he isn't a real man. And faggots are real men, too, and they gotta prove it by bragging and getting drunk and getting laid. Everybody knows that . . . (A beat.) William, are you out of your tiny mind? (Act Two, scene 2)

Her challenging remarks are immediately taken up as men and women, gays and straights, blame each other not only for the AIDS epidemic but for differences in behaviour and attitude. Rather than bring people together, William's illness threatens to become a catalyst in setting off already present divisions between friends and relatives. The anger is not simply directed at each other, but stems from their frustration at being unable to tackle coherently the problem that William's diagnosis presents them with.

Surrounded by their accusations and counter-accusations, William orders them all out of his hospital room, worn out by their fighting. In the following scene, he has begun his own response to their criticism and to his own decision not to speak at the AIDS symposium – his brother Steve arrives with a video camera while William prepares a speech to record. In a direct plea to the audience as well as to the video camera, William urges behavioural change in a personal testimony to the effects of AIDS:

> Hello. My name is William Davis, and I'm dying. I'm dying from a disease they call the Acquired Immune Deficiency Syndrome. I had it for months before I knew what was the matter with me. If you're gay, you could have it too, and not know it. If you think you might have it, please go to a clinic or a doctor and get them to test you straight away. Don't go thinking it's sure to happen to someone else. Learn the warning signs, like persistent fatigue, unexplained weight loss, chronic diarrhoea, swollen lymph glands . . . I don't even know them all myself. But the important thing is to take the responsibility for your own health. If Gay men don't then we may be *forced* to seek treatment. (Act Two, scene 3)

William's testimony visibly affects his straight brother with its honesty, but within a short time, William himself has died. Dr Helbing, informing Dave of William's death, asserts the importance of William's tape – Dave had a test as a result of it, and his result came back as negative. Although William has died, there is hope for the future, and work for the gay community to do in educating and organizing itself.

Andy Kirby's play *Compromised Immunity* was given a first reading with Gay Sweatshop as part of their Times Ten Festival at the Drill Hall Arts Centre in London, in October 1985. In February of that year, the Government had announced that AIDS would not be made a notifiable disease, but that Health Authorities would be given powers to detain AIDS patients if necessary. A month later the House of Lords had their first debate on AIDS. The same year had also seen Gay Sweatshop tour their anti-war play, *Poppies*, by Noël Greig. The company had run into a storm of controversy when the play was presented at the Taliesin Theatre in Swansea and cleaners expressed fears about contracting AIDS if they cleaned up after the company. Local and national newspapers reported the incident, overshadowing the play itself with drama. The situation was finally settled when a medical officer and a union representative explained transmission routes to the cleaners. Yet the fear which had been generated represented the climate created by media stories and insensitive – even counterproductive – government 'information' campaigns.

Compromised Immunity is the story of a straight male nurse, Peter Dennett, as he addresses a lecture theatre about his work with an AIDS patient, Gerry Grimond. In the first scene, Peter directly addresses a fictional audience who were due to be watching a video. Instead, he explains his work as a student nurse, and his first meeting with Gerry at the East London Teaching Hospital. His supervisor, Miss Coates, forewarns the young nurse that Gerry has a reputation as a difficult patient, and Peter's first meeting with his patient is terse and confrontational. Gerry is in a isolation room, and Peter wearing mask and gloves. Their initial response to each other, based on presuppositions they both make about identity, profession and position are gradually peeled away as Peter attempts to understand his patient's anger and frustration at disease and society. Peter also has to struggle with his girlfriend Marie's concerns about his work, and how their relationship is affected. As Peter gets to know Gerry better, he learns about Gerry's ex-lover, Hugh, and delivers a note from Gerry to him. Peter also attempts to get Hugh to visit the hospital. When Gerry is told that Peter is to move to another hospital, he attempts suicide, bringing their friendship and professional relationship into sharp focus. Peter has become more than a nurse – he has become a buddy to Gerry, and this is recognized by the hospital when Peter is assigned to Gerry for a longer period. Part of Peter's learning process is trying to understand Gerry and his world, so he arranges to take Gerry to a gay club but Gerry refuses. Coming back from the club, a young gay man, Ian, tries to pick Peter up, but is persuaded instead to visit Gerry at the hospital. The two become friends: Gerry recognizes a vulnerability in Ian (recently out and just moved to London) and starts helping him plan to find somewhere to stay. Frightened that he had become useless, he is now able to make use of his experience as a gay man. In turn, Ian befriends Gerry and builds up Gerry's social relationship, phoning old friends to let them know about Gerry's hospitalization. Peter and Gerry's relationship is cemented in the Stevie Smith poem 'Black March', with Gerry seeing in Peter his own 'Black March' of destiny. Having come to terms with his own mortality, Gerry is prepared to die peacefully, and Peter's closing address to the audience pays tribute to Gerry's role in teaching him that dying can isolate people, or bring them together.

Compromised Immunity examined many of the fears associated with otherness, how gay men have been compromised not only by the HIV virus but also by the attitudes of society and particularly the medical profession. Both *Compromised Immunity* and *Anti Body* reflect the very real concerns of the time that the medical profession was ill-equipped and often unwilling to deal with a disease that largely affected gay men – traditionally, homosexuality was viewed as an illness and so physical manifestations of illness simply extended the metaphor (in *Anti-Body* the nurse, Dottie, is more horrified at two men embracing than at William's actual physical illness). Peter is frustrated with what medicine can do for Gerry, and at his own attitudes and those of the people around him, although he does advise and help Gerry inform himself as much as possible about AIDS. Dr Helbing also feels the difficulties of working within a profession with little knowledge of how AIDS works or how it might be treated.

Both plays also deal with the necessity to inform, challenge and change people's behaviour and attitudes. Significantly, both plays put prejudice in a historical framework – for William, it is something he has always had to fight against, and Gerry rediscovers a Middle Ages ritual for casting out lepers from a community. He describes the ritualizing of banishment and exclusion:

> They'd take the person into the church and kneel them under a black cloth between two trestles, the ones they put coffins on. Then the priest would say: 'I forbid you ever to enter churches or go into a mill or bakehouse or into any assemblies of people.'[5]

The two plays are similar in story and attitude, reflecting the anger, frustration and confusion which surrounded AIDS at the time. The emphasis that both plays put on self-reliance as a community and the dramatic importance of becoming protagonists rather than victims (particularly in the case of William) helps to balance some of their weaknesses. That they were *necessary* in order to bring the subject to people's attention is itself significant: playgoing is a collective activity, and what both plays called for was collective action to combat the new epidemic. In effect, the plays implicated the audience not just emotionally but as being themselves part of the action – William addresses the camera in his final scene at the same time as he addresses the audience, and Peter Dennett delivers his narrative to the auditorium not just in a lecture hall as indicated in the script but in the theatre where the play is taking place.

It is such implication and interaction which make drama an effective tool in educating and publicizing around AIDS. However, such theatre work is still not properly recognized, either in education or in theatrical environments, and the AIDS crisis of the past decade or so has seen a particular reaction to HIV and AIDS which makes a damaging and disempowering connection with drama – or, particularly, tragedy. The dramatization of AIDS – a 'Camille effect' (after the doomed protagonist of Alexandre Dumas's novel *La Dame aux camélias*) – has become an increasingly used metaphor not simply in drama criticism but within the fields of sociological and medical studies around AIDS. The use of theatrical metaphors in AIDS discourse mystifies rather than clarifies the problems and challenges posed by HIV, reducing those involved to the role of 'spectator' of events with a predetermined, 'tragic' finale.

It is not difficult to understand why the media seek to make AIDS into a stage tragedy, in a world where news reporting, television footage and magazine photojournalism require drama and 'personal interest' to appeal to a mass audience. It is more disturbing when the metaphor of AIDS as theatre becomes used as unanalysed shorthand for progressive rhetoric, disguising the implications such strategies have. In his account of AIDS in America significantly titled *And the Band Played On*, Randy Shilts begins with a list of the 'Dramatis Personae', and describes in his Prologue how 'The story of these first five years of AIDS in America is a drama of national failure, played out against a backdrop of needless death'.[6]

Simon Watney, more critically, has referred to 'the spectacle of AIDS'.[7] Michael Feingold's introduction to an American collection of 'AIDS plays' is unashamedly purple in tone:

> Imagine a play with no protagonist. The action proceeds, some characters suffer unimaginably and die, others in their wake are left bereft, crazed, numbed with shock. The performance goes on, lasting days, months, years. Uncounted numbers participate. The torment continues without explanation and without letup; alleviations are found, but no solutions. The end of the performance is not yet in sight. The main character is still invisible.[8]

The 'leading figure in this terrifying and interminable spectacle' is, of course, AIDS. Even Susan Sontag, the great demystifier of AIDS and metaphors, refers to AIDS as 'illustrating the classic script for plague'.[9]

Tempting though these metaphors may be, they're rooted in misleading and unhelpful presumptions. The first, and most obvious, is that the AIDS crisis is not a piece of theatre, that it is a very real concern that can't be wished away by the closing of a stage curtain. Theatre can be seen as the mirror of life, but it does not dictate the course of life itself. To refer to AIDS as a global drama, a tragedy, is to see it as a pretence, a show. There is no script for AIDS. No actors, no performance. Furthermore, as Michael Bronski has pointed out, its all too easy to see AIDS as drama, as such a metaphor fits in nicely with a view of gay sexuality belonging to 'an old, ingrained, Western cultural tradition, the *Camille* syndrome: the romance of the outlaw, the misunderstood one who may die, but who dies beautifully and with a great deal of pathos and sentiment. Here is the incurable romantic'.[10]

Perhaps a more insidious problem with the 'AIDS as theatre' metaphor is the nature of contemporary theatre itself, divided between spectator and protagonist, actor and audience. In this scenario, not everyone is an actor, a character – the majority must be spectators. In the best tradition of such metaphors associated with illness, Sontag locates a similar narrative in her reading of Jean Giono's 1951 novel *Horseman on the Roof*, which is told 'from the point of view of a traumatised witness, who will be a benumbed survivor'.[11] We can't all be characters in the play – modern theatres demand an audience – and if we're not taking part in this 'drama', then we must be watching it. The metaphor, therefore, results in us becoming passive, inactive. The drama is 'inexorable', unstoppable, predetermined. More concerningly, the major protagonist of this section is not a recognizable character but an archetypal, invisible *villain* – AIDS. It is AIDS that dictates the action, that is the prime mover of the plot. There can be no discourse, no synthesis or antithesis within the drama because the mythical character AIDS has doomed all to destruction, physically and spiritually. Any action by the medical and caring professions, the political and social networks which have sprung up in response to AIDS, are all effectively pissing in the wind. We are invited to witness, not to act. Augusto Boal's criticism of the spectator/protagonist dichotomy is relevant here:

> the world is known, perfect or about to be perfected, and all its values are imposed on the spectators, who passively delegate power to the characters to act and think in their place. In so doing the spectators purge themselves of their tragic flaw – that is, of something capable of changing society.[12]

By accepting the distancing role that this metaphor offers, we are all invited to become AIDS 'victims' in every sense. We are encouraged to accept uncritically medical treatments, viewpoints and definitions. We are encouraged to accept governmental inaction, ineffective educational campaigns, inadequate funding and censorship. Our lives are not our own, are not in our control. What Bronski and John M. Clum refer to as 'the Camille effect' transforms ideas for action into inaction, making us all tragic drama queens, watching and waiting as our collective individual bodies disintegrate or dissipate.

It was precisely to counter such negativity that Larry Kramer, author of the novel *Faggots* and *The Normal Heart*, delivered a speech to a group of approximately 250 men and women at the Gay and Lesbian Community Center in New York on 10 March 1987, nearly four years after he published a landmark article entitled '1,112 and counting' in *The New York Native*. The number in the article's title referred to the statistics on AIDS cases in America at the time, and was carefully worded to elicit a strong response from the gay community. Kramer's speech in 1987 was calculated to achieve the same effect. In January 1982, Kramer had helped to found the Gay Men's Health Crisis (GMHC), an early community response to the AIDS crisis. The internal wrangles and clashes were recorded in his play *The Normal Heart*, and caused him to leave the organization that he had helped to set up. In 1987, however, his tone was one of anger and defiance, hoping to inspire a community response to the AIDS crisis in New York. Two days after his speech, around three hundred people helped him to establish the AIDS Coalition To Unleash Power (ACT-UP), with the original intention of fighting for the release of experimental drugs to help treat people with AIDS. On 24 March, 130 people demonstrated against the Food and Drug Administration (FDA) on Wall Street, the government agency responsible for licensing new drugs. The FDA had approved the release of AZT, an antiviral drug, in only two years, when most drugs would take between eight and ten years to process. The pharmaceutical company Burroughs Wellcome, granted a monopoly over the drug, charged over $10,000 per patient per year, making AZT the most expensive drug ever. The demonstration, designed to draw attention to the FDA's dubious alliance with big business, caused traffic problems for several hours, and an effigy of Dr Frank Young (head of the FDA), which had been built by the theatre practitioner and influential alternative theatre producer Joseph Papp, was hanged in front of Trinity Church. ACT-UP's first demonstration paved the way for a new form of direct action and theatrical manoeuvre which soon crossed over to Britain.

A London ACT-UP chapter was formed in January 1989, with over a hundred people attending the first meeting. A year before, thousands of lesbians and gay men had taken to the streets to protest against what was to become Section 28 of the Local Government Act, and the energy and sense of common purpose generated by the anti-Clause campaign helped to provide a new climate for activism in Britain. The Clause campaign had also seen lesbians and gay men uniting to fight, with connections being made with the trade unions and other sympathetic movements. During the 1970s and early 1980s there had been a general move towards separate campaigning for lesbian and gay men – Section 28, which for the first time in British law criminalized sexual identity, threatened lesbians and gay men together. ACT-UP London became a diverse, non-partisan, non-violent direct action group made up of lesbians, gays, bisexuals and heterosexuals, united in anger and committed to ending the AIDS crisis.

ACT-UP London quickly organized to demonstrate at the annual meeting of Wellcome shareholders, protesting against the price of AZT and the amount of profit being made by Burroughs Wellcome out of the AIDS pandemic. Since then, ACT-UP London have organized dozens of different actions, with targets ranging from the offices of the *Daily Mail*, who printed virulently anti-gay views from their homophobic columnist George Gale, to Benetton for a controversial advertising campaign, to Texaco for enforcing HIV testing for all employees. The demonstrations have frequently been dramatically visual and innovative protests, with props and costumes ranging from a lifesize model of a sheep and an oversize model of a syringe to a camp Statue of Liberty costume. Tactics have included 'dying-in' (where protesters simultaneously 'die' and have their outlines chalked or painted as a symbol of the thousands who've died from AIDS), disrupting meetings and boycotting goods such as Marlboro cigarettes or Texaco petrol, as well as the more mundane but essential groundwork of research and working as a pressure group.

In America, ACT-UP have attracted considerable attention in recognition of their political use of art and spectacle to raise public awareness around HIV and AIDS. Artists such as Barbara Kruger and Keith Haring have produced stunning visual art which carries overtly into political slogans or messages about the AIDS crisis, and ACT-UP sub-groups such as Gran Fury and DIVA TV (Damned Interfering Video Activist Television, a group of video-makers) have devoted themselves to group production of politically useful (essential?) materials. *Let the Record Show*, an art installation project by ACT-UP indicting prominent individuals for their responses (or lack of them) to AIDS, was given space in the new Museum of Contemporary Art in New York, ACT-UP's artworks and influences have been the subject of a number of articles and books, without (necessarily) becoming sanitized as 'art'. The visual aspect of ACT-UP's work has always been recognized and recorded, particularly in America, and such recognition has contributed significantly to widening the audience that ACT-UP's messages can reach.

This recognition has also meant that ACT-UP has had to evaluate its own tactics and manoeuvres, developing its own 'activity aesthetic' as a challenge to mainstream art forms and engaging in a debate with practitioners and theoreticians. Douglas Crimp, an ACT-UP activist and responsible for much of the debate around activist aesthetics, notes: 'The aesthetic values of the traditional art world are of little consequence to AIDS activists. What counts in activist art is its propaganda effect; stealing the procedures of other artists is part of the plan – if it works, we use it'.[13]

Gran Fury, in particular, are 'a band of individuals united in anger and dedicated to exploiting the power of art to end the AIDS crisis'[14] and their poster 'WITH 42,000 DEAD, ART IS NOT ENOUGH, TAKE COLLECTIVE DIRECT ACTION TO END THE AIDS CRISIS' appropriately fuses form with content to describe and illustrate their aims. What becomes important is redirecting artistic energies away from elitist confinement within arts establishments, and channelling those energies to challenge and inform the general public, to highlight negligence, inaction and bigotry, and encourage action and empowerment. Crimp also acknowledges that the AIDS activists' audience will consist of the activist movement itself, because 'AIDS activist graphics enunciate AIDS politics to and for all of us in the movement'.[15] ACT-UP's complementary slogans ACTION = LIFE and SILENCE = DEATH recognize the importance of acting up in order to preserve, enhance and protect life. Moreover, they emphasize the need to design strategies which, when competing in the modern media marketplace, can inspire, inform and educate in as short a time as possible – whether this is in a 'sound-byte' for television or radio, in photographs for newspapers and magazines or in attracting shoppers or workers in the street. Former ACT-UP London member Simon Watney has claimed: 'The AIDS activist aesthetic thus amounts to nothing less than a guerilla semiotics on all fronts, threatening "normality" with a long, sustained, deliberate derangement of its "common sense" '.[16]

Whereas the metaphor of AIDS as theatre can be an impediment to real action, and much AIDS drama has been ignored by mainstream theatre, the theatrical and artistic manoeuvres of groups like ACT-UP have regalvanized political street theatre in a (literal) fight for life, a conclusion also reached by John M. Clum in his book *Acting Gay*: 'The flamboyant, celebratory masking has been transformed into potent performances of unmasking aimed at those who are doing nothing, or less than nothing, about AIDS.[17] The theatrical manoeuvres of AIDS activism recognize a collective body, united in a crisis, and crossing over previous boundaries – according to Crimp, identity is 'wilfully taken on, in defiant declaration of affinity with the "others" of AIDS: queers, women, Blacks, Latinos, drug users, sex workers'.[18] AIDS, normally associated with a single body, affecting 'a patient', is here acknowledged as affecting and infecting larger numbers of people, and affecting society in a significant way. Where Theatre-In-Education has taken theatre around HIV into classrooms, youth clubs and school halls, ACT-UP have taken to the streets. Their very existence is a clarion call to action – 'ACT-UP, Fight Back, Fight AIDS NOW!'

There have been other, more personal responses to the AIDS crisis. In America, the Names Project, where families and friends who knew someone who'd died from AIDS made a section of quilt (an all-American symbol), was displayed at the Mall in Washington D.C. in October 1987. It made concrete the sheer number of people who've died from AIDS, and has since been exhibited (in parts) around the world. As Michael Feingold has written, in the same article where he so graphically described AIDS as a player on a global stage, 'Mourning, privately or collectively, is a beginning of action'.[19]

In fact, for gay men, mourning itself has become a site of resistance. Often excluded – consciously or otherwise – from traditional funerals or mourning ceremonies, we have created our own. The candlelight vigils and readings of names organized every year in Trafalgar Square have become a collective expression of grief. Individually, funerals or memorial services often become the final event which people with AIDS can control or stage manage. In my own play *Dolphins Can Swim* (Chelsea Centre Theatre, 1992), I dealt with a young man rehearsing his own funeral, turning it into a celebration of his own life, and one which he could share with his friends. Gay funerals have mixed camp with grief in ceremonies which celebrate and mourn life and death. As Simon Watney has pointed out:

> gay men have learned to celebrate the achievements of the living, and mourn our dead, *on the terms of our own culture*. Anyone who has heard the frequent juxtaposition of disco-music by Grace Jones or Donna Summer played at AIDS funerals alongside arias from the *Verdi Requiem* or *Der Rosenkavalier* will appreciate this point very well.[20]

At a new centre for people with HIV and AIDS in east London, I have been told that there is a theatre space which will double as a space for funerals and memorial services. The London Lighthouse, a residential centre for people with AIDS in London, often hosts performances and benefits, in a room appropriately named after Ian McKellen, actor and gay campaigner. The ironies inherent in the AIDS crisis are not lost on those involved in it. Our artistic responses to the crisis have been tempered by practicality on every level, without limiting imagination or creativity. With no immediate cure in sight, and limited treatments available, it seems that the AIDS crisis will be with us for some time. If this is the case, then our imaginations will be continually tested and no doubt we shall develop more ways with which to demonstrate anger and grief. However, we can be certain that the most inspirational, direct and meaningful reactions to the AIDS crisis will not come from institutionalized British theatre, which for so long has denied even the existence, and certainly the extent, of the AIDS crisis. Even the writers, including all the major voices of the 1960s, 1970s and 1980s such as Howard Brenton, Caryl Churchill, Sarah Daniels, David Edgar, Howard Barker, Harold Pinter, Timberlake Wertenbaker and John Osborne, do not see AIDS as dramatic material. At the moment, theatrical manoeuvres remain not simply among the most useful artistic responses to the AIDS crisis, but also one of the most necessary, if the body politic is to continue to challenge and celebrate its own ideas and strategies.

Notes

1. Robert Chesley, *Jerker or The Helping Hand*, in *Outfront*, ed. Don Shewey (New York: Grove Press, 1988), scene 9, p. 476.
2. The National AIDS Trust's Youth Initiative, supported by the Health Education Authority, was a series of consultations with over 500 sixth formers in eight different venues around England between November 1990 and March 1991: 'The drama and the video both appeared to have some impact by creating an agenda through which to talk about the topic', although video fared less well than drama (Diane Goodsman's 'Summary of points raised by facilitator led sessions', NAT *Living for Tomorrow*, 1991, p. 32).
3. Dane Court Grammar School in Broadstairs allows sixth formers to train with the Health Promotion Unit of Canterbury and Thanet Health Authorities on a three-day course, and the school provides teaching materials for the HIV Awareness course. See Susannah Kirkman, 'Friendly advice', *Times Educational Supplement*, 31 January 1992.
4. Louise Kelley, *Anti Body*, Act One, scene 2, p. 11, unpublished script. Thanks to Eric Presland and CAIP for making this available.
5. Andy Kirby, *Compromised Immunity*, in *Gay Sweatshop: Four Plays and a Company*, ed. Philip Osment (Methuen, 1989), p. 62.
6. Randy Shilts, 'Prologue', in *And the Band Played On; Politics, People and the AIDS Crisis* (Harmondsworth: Penguin, 1988), p. xxii.
7. Simon Watney, 'The spectacle of AIDS', *October* (winter 1987).
8. Michael Feingold, Introduction to *The Way We Live Now: American Plays & the AIDS Crisis* (New York: Theatre Communications Group, 1990), p. xi.
9. Susan Sontag, *AIDS and Its Metaphors* (Harmondsworth: Penguin, 1990), p. 51.
10. Michael Bronski, 'Death and the erotic imagination', in *Taking Liberties: AIDS and Cultural Politics*, ed. Erica Carter and Simon Watney (Serpent's Tail, 1989), p. 225.
11. Sontag, *AIDS and Its Metaphors*, p. 54.
12. Augusto Boal, *Theatre of the Oppressed* (Pluto Press, 1979), p. 155.
13. Douglas Crimp, in Crimp with Adam Rolston, *AIDS Demo Graphics* (Seattle: Bay Press, 1990), p. 15.
14. Cited in Crimp and Rolston, *AIDS Demo Graphics*, p. 16.
15. Crimp and Rolston, p. 20.

16. Simon Watney, 'Representing AIDS', in *Ecstatic Antibodies: Resisting the AIDS Mythology*, ed. Tessa Boffin and Sunil Gupta (Rivers Oram Press, 1990), p. 190.

17. John M. Clum. *Acting Gay: Male Homosexuality in Modern Drama* (New York: Columbia University Press, 1992), p. 82.

18. Crimp and Rolston, *AIDS Demo Graphics*, p. 18.

19. Feingold, introduction to *The Way We Live Now*, p. xiv.

20. Watney, 'Representing AIDS', p. 166.

Part Two
Codes

Chapter four

Looking for Friends of Dorothy

Well I was talking to a friend
And I was saying:
I wanted you.
And I was looking for you.
But I couldn't find you. I couldn't find you.
And he said: Hey!
Are you talking to me?
Or are you just practising
For one of those performances of yours?
Huh?

Language! It's a virus!
Language! It's a virus!

   Laurie Anderson, 'Language Is a Virus'[1]

Turing: In the long run, all things considered, it's not
breaking the code that matters – it's where you go from
there. That's the real problem.

           Hugh Whitemore, Breaking the Code[2]

MICHAEL Bronski has eloquently pointed in *Culture Clash* that in order to escape the repressive restrictions of mainstream (heterosexual) culture, the gay subculture 'hides, recreates

itself, takes secret or coded forms, and regroups to survive'.[3] Homosexuality has often been presented as a series of codes, dripping with
dark and mysterious meanings, a twilight culture of furtive secrecy.
Articles that showed 'How to spot a Homo'[4] accompanied the
debate around homosexual law reform in the 1960s, and revealed a
prurient interest in the supposed secrecy of homosexuality and its
mythical system of codings and/or signals. The fact that homosexuality, unlike physical characteristics such as colour, *can* be hidden
also means that it has the potential for being revealed – leading not
only to press speculation about famous people's sexuality but also to
the adoption in some quarters of the gay community of 'outing' as a
tactic against closeted male homosexuals or lesbians who attempt to
hide their sexuality while criticizing or punishing others for being
open about theirs. One of the most long-standing traditions surrounding homosexuality is the way in which those who won't or
can't reveal (or come to terms with) their own (homo)sexuality can
use their own privilege or power to persecute those who do choose
to. Whether such people are threatened or genuinely resentful of
sexuality, history has shown that the encoding nature of sexuality
has been used as tool of repression and also security.

Encoding the presentation of (homo)sexuality was essential
to avoid censorship in the British theatre until the abolition of the
powerful role of the Lord Chamberlain – dubbed the 'royal smut-
hound' in many quarters – as a result of the Theatres Act in 1968.
The Lord Chamberlain's traditional role was to see and approve all
scripts in Britain, and to license them as 'suitable' for public performance. In practice, what made the sensitive Lord Chamberlain
squirm most were attacks on the monarchy or the establishment –
an unsurprising foible given that the Lord Chamberlain was himself
appointed from the peerage. The Lord Chamberlain's other pet
hate was what Kenneth Tynan termed 'the bedding-*cum*-liquid-
and-solid-eliminating area'.[5] The presentation of sexuality invariably implied, if not demonstrated, the sexual act itself, and
would frequently attract the Lord Chamberlain's wrathful blue
pencil. In response, authors made sure that homosexuality and
homosexual themes would become encoded or ambiguous, so that
a number of meanings could be read into the text and alluded to.
When a play such as J. P. Ackerley's *The Prisoners of War* (dealing

with a strong homoerotic relationship between its central characters) was given a public licence after a Sunday night showing at the Royal Court Theatre in 1925, it was very much the exception rather than the rule and illustrates the necessity for those codes which Ackerley adopted in the play. The argument for a 'homo*social*' bonding between the two male protagonists obscures what others may see as a less platonic, and more homo*sexual*, innuendo.

The necessity for encoding plays in British theatres became important for both commercial and critical success, and although many studies of gay drama look at the homosexual characters and *content* of historical texts, the study of how these sexualities have been hidden, their codings and semiotics, is also of interest – particularly as sexual identities and categorizations have changed so much over time. A text may have many readings, and no 'true' meaning, even if we can recognize with hindsight that (homo)sexuality has been sublimated, or male homosexual desire or characteristics transferred on to female characters. To study the encoding process is to acknowledge the range of theatrical manoeuvres invented and imagined over time, even if many of these manoeuvres have often led to the same dead-end of the 'closet'. Furthermore, the possibility of encoding and disguising homosexual lifestyle and practice in theatre and the arts has often reflected public concerns and attitudes towards sexuality itself, and the experience of homosexuals off stage. And – albeit somewhat surreptitiously – the potential for encoding and distinguishing such themes has been acknowledged for some time in the theatre, where reputations have been made and broken by public perceptions. The urge to sublimate unpopular or controversial themes has often been an excuse for capitulating to commercial prejudices. Kaier Curtin records a glorious example of such procrastination in his account of homosexuality in American theatre, *We Can Always Call Them Bulgarians*. In 1937, the possibility of Stephen Powys's play *Wise Tomorrow* being filmed by Warner Brothers was commented on by *New York Post* columnist Wilella Waldorf:

> It has been whispered the theme has a touch of Lesbianism about it, which sounds a little odd when you consider that the Warners, presumably, have in mind a picture version

eventually. However, as Samuel Goldwyn or somebody once said, 'We can always call them Bulgarians.'[6]

Waldorf's comments illustrate not only the way in which homosexuality can be wilfully overlooked or disguised, but also the ways in which the coding process can itself be smugly acknowledged. A more disturbing symptom of the encoding process of homosexuality in theatre is the desperate need of some to expose (or imagine) the extent to which homosexuality has been covertly expressed and dealt with in the theatre. In England, claims that the theatre has been run for some time by a homosexual mafia have been given vituperative prominence by stubbornly heterosexual playwrights such as John Obsorne. The presence of prominent homosexuals in British theatre has encouraged those like Osborne who wish to believe that a Masonic club based on a shared sexuality actually controls the West End. If only we did, there might be a very different selection of productions presented. Of course, if homosexuality has been made secret, presented in coded and manipulative forms, then it is only a matter of time before someone excluded by this system of semiotics attempts exclusively to translate or reveal those codes for an unwitting and duped public. In 1963, Martin Taubman of the *New York Times* attempted such an exposé when he was prompted to write some 'Helpful hints on how to scan the intimations and symbols of homosexuality in our theater' after a production of William Inge's *Natural Affection*. Included in the article was a list including the following codes for spotting the spectre of homosexuality in American drama:

> Look out for the male character who is young, handsome, remote and lofty in a neutral way . . .
>
> Be on guard for the male character whose proclivities are like a stallion's.
>
> Beware the husband who hasn't touched his wife for years. . . . Be suspicious of the compulsive slut . . . who represents a total disenchantment with the possibility of a fulfilled relationship between man and woman.
>
> Be alert to scabrous innuendo about the normal male–female sexual relationship.[7]

According to Taubman, everything and everyone was suspect because the codes for homosexuality were themselves so complex and contradictory. Given that the list is so exhaustive, it is surprising that he himself did not come under suspicion. His view is similar in tone and content to an article published in Britain in the same year. The *Sunday Mirror*'s 'How to spot a Homo' (published on 28 April 1963), as we have seen, with its talk of 'silk shirts' and 'hairy sports jackets' perhaps reflected transatlantic concern and paranoia about effeminacy, homosexuality, secrecy and culture. Taubman's article also reflects widespread opinion that homosexuality – being 'unnatural' – can be spotted and catalogued, notably through a series of crude stereotypes. But, more worryingly (for him), it was also seen to be an essentially secretive activity, of which anybody could be 'guilty'. Suspicion naturally graduated towards the theatre, which had a reputation for harbouring, protecting and condoning homosexuality, and which had its own series of codes and semiotics (artificially phrased as 'aesthetics'), both on and off stage. That identity could be complicated by pretence and that theatre could not only imitate but satirize society added to the dilemma about meaning, role and reality. Paradoxically, the pressure from decoders like Taubman leads either to a further encoding, a more complicated set of codes and rituals with which to hide or complicate meaning, or to an explicitness where that which should be hidden becomes brazen, even condoned or celebrated. The more liberal 1960s culture which did away with the antiquated role of the Lord Chamberlain allowed the theatre to become more adventurous in its dealings with homosexuality, as accounts such as Nicholas de Jongh's *Not in Front of the Audience* and Kaier Curtin's *We Can Always Call Them Bulgarians* illustrate. John M. Clum, another chronicler of gay theatre, in his analysis of the changing representation of male homosexuality in modern drama in Britain and America, alludes to the importance of examining the underlying system of codes in drama preceding this period: 'The history of the silences and codes used in the presentation of homosexuality in dramas of the thirties, forties and fifties mirrors the changing position of gay men offstage'.[8] The American gay dramatist Robert Patrick illustrates the same point in his epic cycle of gay plays, *Untold Decades*, where each play examines issues and situations affecting gay men in a particular decade from the 1920s onwards. Each decade provides for different ways in which (homo)-sexual identities might be explored. The whole series itself represents a potted theatrical history of the ways in which gay men have made use of codes and theatricality to disguise, display or demonstrate their private and public lives.

The analogy between codes on and off the stage is an important one, and may help in documenting the ways in which gay men have adopted codes in speech, dress and manner in order to survive, outwit or challenge mainstream culture and ideology. The self-consciousness of performance and role-playing has created elaborate expressions of homo- and hetero-sexuality in Britain. On stage, sexuality often has to be seen via a set of signals, and with reference to homosexuality this most often means signifying deviance from a previously accepted representation of sexual identity. Traditionally, deviance has been signified negatively through all manner of processes, including madness, neurosis, guilt, effeminacy and suicidal tendencies. In practice, this often becomes a variety of stereotypes, so that behaviour signifies identity and type. In his analysis of Mart Crowley's 1968 play *The Boys in the Band* (a play infamous for its bitchy suicidal stereotyping of self-oppressed homosexuals) Nicholas de Jongh directly addresses the issue of the gay stereotype:

> The stereotype is a characteristic form, a caricature of the archetype, by which society identifies members of a group. Such a procedure is achieved by emphasizing and designating a series of signs and behaviours as indices of membership of a particular group. These characteristics may be innate or acquired.[9]

In the theatre, of course, it's not just homosexuals who are stereotyped, although the stereotyping of homosexuality has a particular regulating effect on sexuality and sexual lifestyles. If theatre not only imitates life but presents alternatives, and even promotes the use of imagination, it can also limit and subjugate representation and the imaginative impulse. John M. Clum in *Acting Gay* lists a series of stereotypes used to imply sexuality, including effeminacy, sensitivity, artistic sensibility, misogyny, pederasty, foppishness and isolation. All the stereotypes are recognizable not only in stage portrayals of homsexuality but in dominant images and ideas about male homosexuality in general. For some, these stereotypes might be helpful, especially in regulating and controlling moral, social and sexual 'deviance'. However, even in the most denigrating portrayal of homosexuality, there is an explicit attack on what is arguably the most damaging weapon that can be used against us – silence. Stereotyping allowed the spectre of homosexuality to be discussed, but limited the scope of discourse available. Homosexuality was often seen as a threat either to society or to the family (for example, R. Anderson's *Tea and Sympathy*, John Osborne's *A Patriot For Me* and Mordaunt Shairp's early play *The Green Bay Tree*), and this is a view which very much fits in with society's general perception of homosexuality in the middle of the twentieth century.

The codes used and presented on stage were often largely by homosexual playwrights attempting to conceal their own sexuality (Tennessee Williams's *belles* – for example Blanch DuBois in *A Streetcar Named Desire* – as a projection of his own homosexual desires might be seen as an American example) or by ostensibly heterosexual playwrights dealing with taboo or 'deviant' subjects (Peter Shaffer, John Osborne, Harold Pinter). The stage representation of homosexuality, until the emergence of gay dramas and gay theatre companies in the mid-1970s, generally assumed that its audiences were heterosexual, and the codes used to signify homosexuality on stage were codes assigning deviance from a heterosexual norm, and not indicating (or protecting) a recognizable gay subculture.

One of the reasons for this may be that theatre is an essentially public medium, and so secret codes are exclusive rather than inclusive. The assumption that audiences are largely heterosexual, and the public nature of theatre, mean that codes concerning sexuality can signify only if they are built on a heterosexual consensus between production and audience. The use of codes on stage depends upon their being recognized as codes, and as theatrical 'shorthand'. In order to present successful subtext, codes have to be flagged as meaning something more than the literal – flowers, sensitivity, dark secrets. Off stage, where 'theatrical' shorthand is used in gay circles it is generally used to indicate membership of a homosexual subculture and becomes more complex. I can remember a lecturer in theatre costume and design, giving a talk about how costume is used to signify characteristics on stage, once unwittingly promulgating gay stereotyping by telling my undergraduate drama class that lesbians invariably wore dungarees, and gay men wore ear-rings. In a trendy drama class in the mid-1980s, it turned out that many of the female students wore dungarees and many of the men had ear-rings, although this did not necessarily denote sexual orientation (as was vehemently expressed at the time!).

As on stage, the homosexual subculture has often been encoded off stage by inference and euphemism, relating to membership of a circle, coterie or family. The title of this chapter refers to the 1939 cult film *The Wizard of Oz*, starring camp icon Judy Garland as the young girl, Dorothy, who gets swept away from her home in Kansas and taken to the fabulous land of Oz. Garland has had a long and close connection with gay men as a camp icon, and it now seems appropriate that the Stonewall riots – the first flowering of Gay Pride – occurred on the night of her burial on 27 June 1969, as drag queens mourned her death. Garland's famous song from *The Wizard of Oz*, 'Somewhere over the rainbow', has been called 'the gay national anthem'.[10] To be a 'friend of Dorothy' is to be part of the circle of Dorothy's friends, i.e. gay men, and is often used in identifying a group of gay men in a hostile (or potentially hostile) setting. Ask for the 'friends of Dorothy', and they'll see you're all right. Dorothy's friends could also be referred to as 'one of the family', 'one of ours', 'one of us' or a 'sister'. Such terms are generally inclusive, welcoming, an acknowledgement of homosexuality. Gay slang and Polari have numerous phrases and terms to identify a 'queen', and in the past terms such as 'molly', 'mary-anne' and 'queen' have been used as terms of endearment and inclusion. The inclusive terms act in sharp opposition to the derogatory abuse and 'queer-bashing' that are often used against homosexuals, and define an alternative identity which emphasizes gay community and belonging.

Codes and forms which indicate homosexuality are numerous and have changed (are changing) over time. They vary from the brazen (pin badges exclaiming 'I'm Gay – Fuck You') to the more genteel and ingenious. Such codes reflect the attitudes and regulations of their time. At the end of the nineteenth century, Oscar Wilde and his circle of friends wore green carnations, which became associated not only with aestheticism but also with his homosexuality. It was a badge already associated with homosexuality in Paris, and Neil Bartlett notes that:

> The little green flower is evidence of far more than apocryphal satorial outrage. Its perfume lingers; by wearing it Wilde ceased to be an individual homosexual with a flair for creating his own public image, and subscribed to a homosexual fashion. He declared himself to be one of an anonymous group of men for whom the wearing of the green carnation *meant* homosexuality.[11] [Bartlett's italics]

The green carnation came to signify the wearer's sexuality, and it is the colour itself which is also important. In her book *Another Mother Tongue*, Judy Grahn examines an old warning from her high school, 'Never wear green on Thursdays', which was taken to indicate that the wearer was homosexual. In her intriguing explanation, Grahn cites the anthropologist Margaret Murray, who believed that prior to the arrival of the Celtic tribes in Britain and other parts of Europe, the land was inhabited by a people known as the 'Fairies', whose primary colour was green. In addition, Thursday was seen as an important ritual day for the fairies and, later, for witches, being the Maid Diana's day. Grahn concludes with a personal theory:

> So I could begin to understand the story underlying my high school taboo about wearing the colour green on Thursday: The green-wearing Fairy people and the Celtic wise women and wizards had used Lesbian and Gay sex rites in ceremonies held especially on Thursdays and had been heavily punished, murdered, publicly terrorized for it. . . . So the strange little warning phrase of never wearing green on Thursday lest you be taken for one of them creates a bond with them over the centuries.[12]

Grahn's explanation may seem unlikely (even if many of us might like to believe it), but the importance of such folklore lies in the way that meanings are attached to significations, and Grahn goes on to weave cross-cultural traditions together in order to explain another infamous indicator of homosexuality, the 'pinky ring'. Grahn emphasizes the metaphysical aspect, largely spiritual in tone, of this particular signifier. Ordinarily a ring worn on the little finger, its position on the hand relates in some traditions to Mercury and Woden, gods of change and transumutability. According to the ancient Native American tradition, pinky rings might also relate to a story about a pacifist shaman who had a small purple spot (the colour purple has also long been associated with homosexuality) on his left hand, and whose murder by his tribespeople cursed them all as warmongers.[13]

Perhaps one of the most coherent systems of codification in the modern gay community is the series of 'hanky codes' and colours used by some gay men as theatrical shorthand to signify sexual preference and desire. Instead of the time-consuming negotiations and love-songs that might accompany more traditional forms of courting, a cursory glance at the back of a pair of 501s is enough to judge the wearer's sexual compatibility. The hanky code works on the simple positioning and colour of a handkerchief in the back pocket of the wearer. A handkerchief in the left-hand pocket indicates that the wearer is an 'active' exponent, and in the right-hand pocket that the wearer 'receives' the activity. A dark blue handkerchief indicates anal sex, so when worn on the left indicates the desire to fuck, and on the right the desire to be fucked. Similarly, a light blue hanky indicates oral sex – worn on the left, to be fellated, on the right it means to fellate (technical definitions of who is 'active' and who is 'passive' in oral intercourse could lead to a great deal of unnecessary semantics). Other colours include yellow (for pissing), black (for sado-masochism) red (for fisting), with more elaborate signs including gold lamé for star-fucking (sex with a celebrity). The system of hanky codes is so mythically complex that gay sex shops often issue lists of what each colour means, with some colours having different shades meaning entirely different expectations. The system does have its drawbacks. Those who, like myself, are colour blind could find themselves in some very awkward situations. And the coding system extends beyond the mere use of handkerchiefs – for example, a small teddy bear indicates a penchant for cuddling. The way keys are worn (left or right) can also indicate the sexual role adopted, and coloured bootlaces likewise. The 'hanky code' is of most use in bars and clubs, where the decorum for picking up passing trade is a system which emphasizes body language and ritual over conversation and small-talk. It is ironic that neckerchiefs, now back in vogue, might be misread entirely by different groups of people.

The codes by which gay men can identify each other and their demands are analogous to the ways in which traditional dramatic subtexts are signalled or implied in productions. Signs and signals disclose information while protecting individuals or communities, working to identify signallers with signal readers by association, inclusion and exclusion. In the 1970s, the pop group Village People adopted a coded form of dress which both identified them as gay (adopting the costumes of gay characters – the Workmen, the Leatherman, the Military Man and so on) but also used those encoded signals to project a theatricality which could be seen as appealing to both hetero- and homosexuality. Part of the presentation was the way in which they encoded themselves theatrically as (reconstructed) gay identities.

One of several such devices, hankies reveal a system of identification and recognition exclusive to the gay community, continuing a tradition of semiotics akin to theatrical metaphors which indicate, protect and communicate identity and practice. Signs indicating homosexuality such as green carnations, brown suede shoes (in the early and middle part of the twentieth century thought to denote homosexuality), pinky rings and ear-rings (gay men traditionally wear ear-rings in the right ear) have helped to contribute a language of metaphors and signals to the gay community which enrich and enliven its culture, and also play an important part in creating and affirming gay sensibility. To be out is to be in the encoding system, from acknowledging a knowing wink or style to extravagant displays that complicate and encode meanings. In turn, the encoding process of homosexuality gives meaning to heterosexual coding systems – wedding rings, ceremonies and courting procedures need *another* system in order to define themselves and to enrich them with meanings. The clumsy attempts of journalists such as Howard Taubman may have correctly guessed that there were homosexual semiotics on stage and in society, but he ultimately failed to recognize either what they were or their true significance in gay culture(s).

Notes

1. 'Language Is a Virus', from the soundtrack *Home of the Brave* by Laurie Anderson, © 1986 Difficult Music/BMI.

2. Hugh Whitemore, *Breaking the Code*, Act II, scene viii, about the gay scientist Alan Turing who cracked the German Enigma code. Produced at the Yvonne Artaud Theatre, Guildford, and later at the Theatre Royal, Haymarket, 1986. Published by Amber Lane Press, 1987.

3. Michael Bronski, *Culture Clash: The Making of Gay Sensibility* (Boston: Southend Press, 1984), p. 3.

4. 'How to Spot a Homo', article in the *Sunday Mirror*, 28 April 1963, cited in Stephen Jeffrey-Poulter, *Peers, Queers and Commons* (Routledge, 1991).

5. Kenneth Tynan, 'The royal smut hound', in *Look Back in Gender*, ed. Michelene Wandor (Methuen, 1987), p. 74.

6. Wilella Waldorf, 'Edith Barrett to play a role in "Wise Tomorrow"', *New York Post*, 17 September 1937, cited in Kaeir Curtin, *We Can Always Call Them Bulgarians* (Boston: Alyson Publications, 1987), p. 218.

7. Howard Taubman, 'Modern primer: helpful hints to tell appearances from truth', *New York Times*, 28 April 1963, sec. 2, p. 1, cited in John M. Clum, *Acting Gay* (New York: Columbia University Press, 1992), p. 176.

8. John M. Clum, preface to *Acting Gay*, pp. xi–xii.

9. Nicholas de Jongh, *Not in Front of the Audience* (Routledge, 1992), p. 134.

10. Bronski, *Culture Clash*, p. 56. Bronski attributes the quotation to lesbian feminist singer Holly Near, who ended her set at the 1979 lesbian and gay march on Washington with the song.

11. Neil Bartlett, *Who Was That Man?* (Serpent's Tail, 1988), p. 50.

12. Judy Grahn, *Another Mother Tongue: Gay Words, Gay Worlds* (Boston: Beacon Press, 1984), p. 81.

13. Grahn, p. 14.

Chapter five

A Cinderella Among Languages

Nantee dinarlee: The omee of the carsey
Says due bionc peroney, manjaree on the cross
We'll have to scarper the jetty in the morning,
Before the bonee omee of the carsey shakes his doss.

Polari busker's song[1]

GAY subculture has always had its own phrases and idioms, coded conversations and expressions that conceal as much as they reveal. From pick-ups asking for a light to exclusively gay expressions, there have always been a variety of gay lingos dependent on time and place. Yet it is in Polari that we see the most concerted effort to create not so much an entire language but certainly a gay vocabulary of coded expressions and words.

Polari (also Parlyaree, Parlary) is the most comprehensive extant form of gay slang, comprising all sorts of odds and ends ranging from rhyming slang and circus backslang to Romany, Latin, and criminal cant. Polari is still spoken by those queens and circus people who can remember it (or piece enough together for a conversation), although perhaps its high renaissance was during the 1950s and 1960s when it was popularized in the mainstream by the larger than life characters of Julian and Sandy in the BBC Radio series *Round the Horne*. Polari is very much a secret language, designed to be used when conversations are to be kept private from eavesdroppers, be they straight queer-bashers, nosy friends or *Lili Law* (the police). Polari – originating from the theatrical *Parlyaree* – is best described as a mish-mash of expressions and words thrown together to make a semi-comprehensible glossary. As the indefatigable chronicler of slang, Eric Partridge, pointed out in 1950 in one of the first-ever attempts to account for Palyaree's popularity and history: 'Parlyaree, then, is a glossary, a vocabulary, not a complete language. Little remains. Even that little may disappear'.[2] As a gay theatrical manoeuvre, Polari represents one of the most accomplished, and least acknowledged, achievements, and also one which has the longest history. As a spoken language, it has gradually disappeared with every speaker who could have passed it on, so that what we now piece together of the language is frustratingly limited, almost to the point of nostalgia. However, the history and culture of Polari and its speakers also reveal much about gay subculture throughout the ages. As gay journalist Peter Burton has written in his autobiographical *Parallel Lives*, 'Such Polari as survives is that which is handed down from one generation of queens to another (incidentally giving us at least one "living" link with our homosexual past)'.[3]

Gay slang, and peculiarly homosexual phraseology, dates back to at least the eighteenth century, and the involvement of the gay subculture with the criminal underworld. The homosexual subculture of the eighteenth century mixed with the thieves, prostitutes and travellers, producing a rich cross-fertilization of customs, phrases and traditions. These marginalized sections of society often found themselves frequenting the same taverns, and living adjacent to each other in the towns and cities. As the Industrial Revolution dramatically changed settlement patterns, and more people drifted to the larger towns, the scope for the development of communities based on a variety of interests mushroomed as more and more people travelled away from rural villages or communities in search of work and opportunity (of one sort or another). The growth of molly houses, and the emergence of the 'molly' identity in the eighteenth century, accompanied the adoption of codes and phrases common to an emerging homosexual subculture, borrowing largely from the cant of thieves, rogues and pickpockets. In his account of the gay subculture in England between 1700 and 1830, Rictor

Norton notes that homosexuals identified as 'mollies, molly-culls, mollying culls and mollying-bitches'.[4] 'Cull' was adapted from thieves' cant, and meant 'mate', or simply 'bloke' (although alternatively it could mean testicles!). Norton also lists words which would have been used by the mollies, and which were in common usage by thieves, such as *mish* ('shirt'), *poll* ('wig'), *Margery-prater* ('hen'), *Queer-Ken* ('prison house'), *stampers* ('shoes') and *shap* ('hat'). It is easy to imagine why petty criminals might develop their own secret language in order to hide their subterfuge and criminal activity from prying ears, and such secret languages would also have enabled them to discuss illicit and/or morally ambiguous or licentious behaviour. This early flowering of codes connected with lifestyle and behaviour feeds into the later development of Parlyaree as the language of travelling showmen in the nineteenth century, and ultimately into gay Polari in the late twentieth century.

Cant, the 'thieves' Latin', is thought to have travelled with the gypsies into eastern Europe in the fourteenth century, through to Italy and western Europe early in the fifteenth century, and ultimately reached Britain by at least the late fifteenth century. As it travelled through different countries and traditions, it changed and evolved as any living language might. The word 'queer' itself demonstrates how such phrases might then have developed further from the thieves' Latin. From 'quire' or 'quyer' in the sixteenth century it had changed to 'quier' or 'quere' by the seventeenth century, but was always associated with meanings of 'bad', 'inferior', 'base'. By the nineteenth century, it had come to signify 'tipsy', 'ill', 'unfavourable': it was later associated with prostitution and, by the twentieth century, with homosexuality.[5]

Ninety per cent of Parlarey, the travelling showmen's language, appears to be derived from the *lingua franca*, or the Italianate vocabulary of eighteenth-century itinerant actors and nineteenth-century costermongers, cheapjacks and showmen. The mutable word 'Parlarey' itself appears to come from the Italian verb *parlare*, meaning 'to speak'. Various spellings of the word exist, including 'Parlyaree', 'Parlaree', 'Palary' and 'Parlarey'. Generally, it is 'palarie' that is taken as the verb, meaning 'to speak'. The first reference to the language appears in Henry Mayhew's *London Labour and the London Poor*, volume iii, no. 43, published in

1851, which states that 'The showmen have but lately introduced a number of Italian phrases into their cant language'.[6] John Bee's *Dictionary* of 1823 records the first Parlyaree term, but Eric Partridge agreed with a source of his, R. Crompton Rhodes, that Parlyaree was already well established with itinerant actors and showmen throughout the eighteenth century, and gave his own reason as to why this should be: 'It was among showmen and strolling players that parlyaree originated, partly in self protection; actors and actresses, especially if itinerant, being a despised class until late in the nineteenth century'.[7] The circus adopted much of the Parlyaree terminology, mixing it with backslang and rhyming slang, and in many ways kept the language alive into the twentieth century, after strolling players ceased to exist in meaningful numbers. By now, the vocabulary had expanded to include words such as *bona* ('face'), *omee* ('man', later to become *omie*), *pollone*, *polone* or *palone* ('woman'), *chavies* or *felliers* ('children'), and *carsey* ('house'). In a culture besotted with ready cash and making deals, it is only natural that there should be many terms relating to money, and this is indeed the case: *dinarly* ('money', possibly from the Spanish *dinero*, the Italian *dinaro* or, via the gypsies, the Persian *dinar*), *nanty metzes* ('penniless') and *parker* ('to pay out') serving as some examples. Parlyaree also had its own set of numbers, which from one to ten were *una*, *dewey*, *tray*, *quattro* (*quater*), *chinker*, *say*, *setter*, *otter*, *nobba* and *daiture*.

As theatrical language developed to include phrases particularly with the theatre and performances of one kind or another, so Parlyaree also reflected its own peculiar heritage. Specifically theatrical Parlyaree included phrases such as *joggering omee* ('street musician'), *slang a dolly to the edge* (to show and work a marionette on a small platform outside the performance booth in order to attract an audience) or *climb the slang-tree* (to perform on stage). *Nanty dinarly* ('having no money') also had a peculiarly theatrical translation in the phrase 'There's no treasury today, the ghost doesn't walk'.

In his account of touring with Paddy O'Flynn's circus in western Ireland, *Sons of Sawdust*,[8] the early twentieth-century artist Edward Seago included a glossary of backslang and other terms used by showmen, illustrating how many Parlyaree terms have actually moved into popular usage. *Balonie* ('nonsense'), *barney* ('fight'), *bevie* ('pub' or 'tavern'), *clobber* ('clothes'), *gaffer* ('showman'), *gag* (a clown's joke), *konk* ('nose'), *scarper* or *to do a Johnny Scarper* ('escape') and *on your tod* ('by yourself') are all listed and can be seen as feeding both into Parlyaree and into more conventional modern usage. Many of the terms are easily recognizable in contemporary Irish speech. Seago also records phrases and terms peculiar to the circus tradition and activities: *bearer* (supporter in an acrobatic act), *barker* (the 'thumper' outside a show, sometimes the ringmaster), *flattie* or *gillie* (a member of the audience), *flip-flap* (an acrobatic trick), *pig* ('elephant'), *ponging* ('somersaulting') and *slobberswing* (a complete circle of the horizontal bar). I am told that the circus still uses backslang and Parlyaree, sometimes providing a cross-over between the gay community and circus performers. The continued use of Parlyaree in a professional context testifies to its usefulness as shorthand or code.

By the mid twentieth century, Polari had emerged as a recognizably gay form of slang and was being used by the gay community to communicate in code in elaborate forms. As early as 1910, 'Xavier Mayne', an American writer, referred to a gay vocabulary in *The Intersexes*.[9] Words such as *trade* and *ecaf* (backslang for 'face', shortened to *eek*) became part of gay subculture, a mixture of camping about and self-protection against unwelcome revelations in public. Even where Polari wasn't spoken as a secret language, odd words invariably referred to homosexual practices, lifestyle or interests. As the historian Jeffrey Weeks has pointed out, 'Much of the argot is highly esoteric, known only to a few homosexuals, but a large number of words are absorbed into the daily vocabulary of homosexuals'.[10] And this vocabulary, although often bawdy and crude, also reached beyond the simple homo*sexual* and into the homocultural. In his brief analysis of 'Parlare as a second language', Oscar Watson comments further:

> In Britain, the hundred or so words that made up working Palarie provided a surprisingly rich patois for a few years during the fifties that described much more than just sex. It provided a collective security and arrogance to use a mode of speech indentifiable only by initiates.[11]

Although Watson might underestimate both Parlyaree's history, and its durability, the 1950s and 1960s certainly did provide a boom period for the flowing of gay Polari. At a time when homosexual clubs were emerging in secret, and law reform around sexuality was being seriously considered by Parliament and the nation, it seems appropriate that Polari should rear its irreverent head as a code for an exciting and important period in gay history. It was during this time that *zhoosing your riah* (fixing your hair) and *trolling to a bijou bar* (going out to a club) became popular phrases in homosexual circles. Terms such as *naff* (meaning 'bad', supposedly from the initials Normal As Fuck) and *TBH* ('To Be Had') also became common, in the most literal sense. The influence of gypsies, tramps and thieves had created a secret post-war argot which accompanied a sense of confidence and the thought that things were *happening* for gay people. In short, Polari became an appropriate theatrical manoeuvre with which to confuse and confound the *naff omees* (straight men) when the *dirt* was being *dished* (gossip being recounted).

Peter Burton's rare account of life with the Polari *hommes* in *Parallel Lives* is of interest not simply because of its account of the language of Polari, but also for the description of the clubs and culture in which it flourished. He conjures up the music and mood of the period, which fed into the Polari culture. Burton also acknowledges that the code he cherished may not have been as secret as his *gaggle* of friends might have liked to think:

> Though we liked to think that no one knew what we were talking about as we polaried away to each other, as we shrieked at full volume about the bona bit of rough trade we'd nearly *blagged* (picked up) the night before, it now seems obvious that any naff worth his salt must have had a pretty good idea of what it was all about. If nothing else, the use of the world 'girl' (term of affection) with which every sentence seemed to end must have made all clearly apparent.[12]

It's from these queens and *bona omies* of the period that much of the Polari still used is handed down, and it is they who remember the language as alive and relevant. Terms which are now used to describe gay life – *cottage* ('public toilets'), *trolling* ('cruising') and *bona* ('good') were made popular during the late 1950s and 1960s in homosexual coteries.

The most famous and popular use of Polari came with the 1960s BBC Radio series *Round the Horne*, which invented the characters of Julian and Sandy, two out-of-work actors who 'made do' with a series of odd jobs and occupations. Jules and Sand, played with camp aplomb by Kenneth Williams and Hugh Paddick, developed a cult following, and the catch phrases 'Ooo, 'inee bold!' and 'How bona to vada your dolly old eek' became well used by naffs and queens alike. The series, written by Marty Feldman and Barry Took, started in 1965 and went out on BBC Radio at the prime time of 2.30 p.m. on Sundays. Unquestionably camp as the proverbial Christmas, Julian and Sandy both titillated and astounded listeners with double (quadruple) innuendoes ('Did that have a second meaning?' 'I don't think it had a first, luv'). As one commentator, Keith Howes, has written about the endearing Jules and Sand:

> They straddled the old and the new concepts of homosex-
> uals: the camp repartee, full of sexual innuendo crossed with
> an assertiveness and strong self-identity. Like the rest of
> *Round the Horne*, Jules and Sand brought into question, as
> the Goons had done, the British obedience to codes of dress,
> behaviour, patriotism, manliness and femininity. They
> became the popular idea of the male gay couple.[13]

Jules and Sand were nothing if not versatile. The series presented the couple in a variety of different situations and occupations – sketches entitled 'Bona Homes and Landscape Gardens', 'Bona Bijou Tourettes', 'Bona Prods' and 'Keep Britain Bona' to name but a few – and made self-conscious use of camp and Polari. Feldman's knowledge of circus, combined with Williams's own experience of the theatre and its language, created a broad homosexual/theatre argot imbued within a strong liberal sensibility.

Like Polari, the radio series loses something in translation, but an extract might show not only the sense of the language Polari, but also the daring smut associated with Julian and Sandy. Hearing it all again in the 1990s, we might still wonder how they got away with it all (or do we just have smuttier minds these days?). In a memorable sketch entitled 'Bona Seances', Kenneth Horne visits Jules and Sand, otherwise known by their professional names 'Madame Bona' and 'The Great Omiepalonie Natural Sensitive':

Jule: I am occupied by your actual mystic forces.

Sand: He is, he's occupied. Frequently. He's got the telepathy, you see. Let your waves blend with his, Mr Horne, and he will reveal all, won't you, Jule?

Jule: Gladly.

Sand: Gladly. It's a gift with him. Some have got it, some haven't. And he's got it. By George, he's got it.

Jule: Now then, how would you like me to prognosticate? Shall we try the ouija?

Sand: Yes, get out your ouija. Let's have a palary with the spirits. Come on, all sit round and hold hands. You sit next to me, Mr Horne. It's all right, don't worry, Jule'll soon be going off.

Jule: Yes, I do, you know, I go right off.

Sand: Pull yourselves together now, nish the chat. He's going into his trance. Are the vibrations favourable, Jule?

Jule: Oh, bona, yes.

Sand: Are you off now?

Jule: Yes, I'm one step beyond.

Sand: Oh, you go, Jule, don't worry about us, we'll be all right on our own. He's going, he's going! He's coming back again. What do you want, Jule?

Jule: I forgot to leave a note for the milkman.[14]

The scene illustrates the mixing of Polari ('nish the chat') with camp humour and innuendo, with Kenneth Horne acting, as always, the straight man (literally). Yet the show was also daring – at the beginning of this particular scene, Sand is identified at the Great Omipalonie, 'omipalonie' meaning 'homosexual' in Polari. Moreover, there is even a play on Horne's own (ostensibly straight) sexuality – the advertisement for 'Bona Seances' was allegedly seen in *Physique Pictorial*, which Kenneth Horne claims to buy for the 'gardening section'. The play on and blurring of Horne's supposed 'normality' continues throughout the series. As the characters developed, Horne himself began to use Polari, causing the probing Jules and Sand to wonder 'where he picks it up' or 'where he spends his evenings'. Significantly, the camp banter between Jules and Sand, together with their cryptic comments, endeared them to a largely heterosexual audience during the late 1960s, as homosexual law reform was about to be passed. Although Paddick and Williams's effeminacy is appealing, criticisms from some quarters emphasize their crude stereotyping:

> despite their fine scripts and positive images, they opened up the door and in swept camp characteristics a la mode. Every Grayson or Shane . . . every D-J cry of 'ducky' does have a link back. A box of delights was opened up by Julian and Sandy and camp – which has existed for as long as We have – was ritualized.[15]

The conclusion here seems to me to be overdramatic: Williams, Paddick, Feldman and Took did not invent either Polari or camp, and it is certain that all over Britain queens were acting camper, and speaking Polari much more, than was being represented on the radio. To become paranoid or censorious about representations such as those characterized by Jules and Sand damages our own perspectives on what is and isn't dangerous or homophobic to present. To blame Jules and Sand for the 'ritualization' of camp stereotypes is to miss both the humour of the series (they *are* funny) and to be damagingly precious about our own self-image and expected gender loyalties. Furthermore, it is not the characters of Julian and Sandy who are being laughed at and neither is their language being derided; Horne accepts (on behalf of the listening audience) both their sexuality and their behaviour. What is being sent up and questioned are the conventional wisdoms of normality and 'straight society'. Jules and Sand are never deterred or put down for their escapades, but instead find themselves in a variety of bizarre situations which naturally invite camp imitation and/or implicit criticism. The code of Polari, on National radio, was used to filter all manner of information on homosexual lifestyle and activity, and constantly alluded to *Lilly Law* (our old friends the agents of the law) and the dangers that Jules and Sand, as *omiepalones* of the world, were forced to deal with.

Jules and Sand, the fictional exponents of sharp wit and Polari, presented not only a gay code but also a form of gay self-defence and security. Although their humour was gentle, Polari off the airwaves and in the salons could be used mercilessly against an intended victim. As Peter Burton testifies, in real life:

> polari had about it a particularly brittle, knife-edged feel. Nothing – in my chicken days – was more daunting than an encounter with some acid-tongued bitch whose tongue was so sharp it was likely to cut *your* throat. These queens, with the savage wit of the self-protective, could be truly alarming to those of us of a slower cast of mind. Many's the occasion I've sat thinking of the devastating replies I could have delivered. By then, though, it was always too late.[16]

Polari became part and parcel of the wise-cracking bitchery between queens, used by them against *naff omies*. In this context, what Peter Burton might have feared follows the long tradition which associates homosexuals with their *bona lavs* ever since Oscar Wilde perfected his elegant put-downs and acid-drops.

Polari as a language continued, and continues in some areas, to change and grow, losing words and terms and picking up others along the way. It became associated with local dialects, so that to speak of a 'true' Polari is inaccurate, as Polari forms differed throughout Britain. It was and still is largely an urban language, reflecting the character of the communities it belongs to. And Polari was never just confined to the land-loving townsfolk. The sea queens – homosexuals in the navy or engaged on sea-cruises – took the language over the ocean waves with them. Riding the seven seas, they varied the language even more, borrowing naval terms and slang to broaden the vocabulary, so that today a distinct difference can be made between sea-Polari and land-Polari.

Such different histories eventually weave together into an almost mythical, fabulous (very nearly lost or Atlantean) gay language. The changing face of Polari has meant that some original Polari terms have changed their meaning somewhat, and become modern in an irregular manner: *bevie* originally meant a tavern or pub, and not a drink. As indicated earlier, many true Polari terms have fallen into common gay usage – *trade* ('sexual partner'), *cottage* and *troll* being some popular examples. Polari has also lent its words to the gay publications such as *Bona* (a 1970s gay soft-porn magazine) and *Varda* (an early 1990s gay freebie). Translated into busking songs and oral histories, its bastardized nature has always lent it a mercurial quality which makes it both charming and frustrating.

Polari's transient qualities, however, have meant that many of the terms are forgotten, or are simply not applicable any more. A language so rooted in its subculture reflects the passage of time and events. The necessary secrecy which accompanied Polari has meant that it never gained a common or universal parlance, and with so few successful attempts at retaining modern gay culture, let alone reclaiming past traditions, it is perhaps unsurprising that the *bijou clubs* and *bevies* no longer sing with the sound of the *bona* Polari *lavs*. Such attempts as are continually being made to reclaim and rediscover the art of *parlying* Polari are invariably small-scale and eclectic.

As a code, Polari has worked very well, both intriguing and misleading eavesdroppers of the magic language. Its history, or collection of histories, has frequently joined with histories of other minority groups – the Romanies, criminal 'underworld', circus showpeople, travelling entertainers and so on. As well as providing a source of amusement for many listeners to *Round the Horne*, Polari helped to protect and affirm homosexual identity, most significantly during the 1950s and 1960s, when gay culture was becoming more visible and law reform imminent. Has Polari then served its purpose as a gay code with little more to offer than a nostalgic (or academic) interest? Does it have a future?

It is true to say that there is a fascination about Polari, and not simply from the gay community. As part of gay and theatrical history, it certainly deserves more attention, and is an important part of what might be seen as a cross-cultural heritage. Its disappearance in gay circles during the early days of gay liberation has been put down by some to its male-orientated puns and put-downs, as well as the more assertive demands of gay liberation. The tactics of gay politics at that time were demanding not mere codings but explicit declarations of sexuality and political intent. The state, law and Church needed to be challenged, something which Polari could not (explicitly) do. Polari's secrecy excluded it from the more visible and forceful gay culture of the 1970s, riding on the back of the pink pound. The harsh 1980s found no room for Polari either, and the nostalgia seen in the pop music scene and marketing strategies of the early 1990s (the revival of 1970s groups such as Boney M, Sister Sledge, Abba and Gloria Gaynor) has arrived when most of Polari and Polari speakers have disappeared. As Oscar Watson has observed: 'Other culturally identifiable social sub-groups support and allow their slangs to develop and grow as a way of maintaining an identifiable unity amongst their members – the same is not true of Palarie'.[17]

However, all is not despair for Polari. It is certainly still used by circus folk, and older queens are known to practise it. There is something of a renaissance with the Sisters of Perpetual Indulgence using 'High Polari' during rituals, blessings and celebrations in place of Latin. American slang shows how language changes and is adopted for particular circumstances and situations, but, as Bruce Rogers's glossary of over twenty thousand gay slang terms illustrates, it lacks the long and mysterious history of Polari.[18] American gay slang does share certain properties with Polari, as Rodgers notes in his introduction to *The Queen's Vernacular*: 'Slang is social protest, used to deflate the hypocrisy of nice-sounding labels that mean nothing to the people who use them. Slang is also the expression of the underdog – it is always aimed against the establishment.[19]

Language has often been a battleground in the history of gay politics, and definitions and redefinitions of sexuality and lifestyle have constantly had to be renegotiated as the meaning of identity changes in accord with circumstances and situations. Current debates about reclaiming language, and the creation of politically correct (sanctioned) phraseology, have shown how territorial people can be about language. We are what we speak. If it's claimed that the rise in queer politics encompasses a street language –

queerspeak, a mixture of jargon, political rhetoric and aggressive self-promotion – then the cultural heritage found in Polari gives strength and feeling to the reality of creating, or re-interpreting, ourselves linguistically. If Polari was originally created for self-protection, it can now be valued for its sense of history and tradition, and acknowledged to be camp, extra-ordinary fun. Its own history is a magical tapestry of half-truths and mercurial mushrooming, a theatrical manoeuvre that has lasted – in one form or another – for nearly two hundred years.

With such a fairytale history, it seems appropriate that the first study of Parlyaree, by Eric Partridge in 1950, originated as a few notes transformed into a Christmas card which he sent out to his friends. The piece was then later eventually published with the suitably charming subtitle 'Cinderella among languages'. If Polari is indeed the magical Cinderella of languages, then perhaps it is appropriate to note that she's still waiting for a fairy godmother to transform her into a princess.

Notes

1. Letter to Eric Partridge from Herbert Seaman, 'learned in the ways of theatre, music-hall, side-show', quoting a song recited to him by Mr Dai Griffith, current among street buskers of the period (1950) (Eric Partridge, *Dictionary of Slang and Unconventional English*, ed. Paul Beale (Routledge & Kegan Paul, 8th edition, 1984). Roughly translated, the song means 'We've got no money, the landlord of the pub says he's owed a penny by everyone, and the food's been got by cheating. We'll have to leave in the morning before the landlord throws us out.' Of course, it loses something in the translation.

2. Eric Partridge, 'Parlyaree – Cinderella among languages', in *Here, There and Everywhere: Essays upon Language* (Hamish Hamilton, 1950).

3. Peter Burton, *Parallel Lives* (GMP, 1985), p. 41.

4. Rictor Norton, *Mother Clap's Molly House: The Gay Subculture in England 1700–1830* (GMP, 1992), p. 103.

5. Partridge, *Here, There and Everywhere*.

6. Cited in Partridge, *Here, There and Everywhere*, p. 116.

7. Partridge, *Here, There and Everywhere*, p. 117.

8. *Sons of Sawdust – With Paddy O'Flynn's Circus in Western Ireland*, written and illustrated by Edward Seago (Putnam, 1924).

9. 'Xavier Mayne', *The Intersexes* (Florence, 1919).
10. Jeffrey Weeks, *Coming Out* (Quartet Books, 1977), p. 42.
11. Oscar Watson, 'Palare as a second language', *Square Peg*, issue 27, 1990.
12. Burton, *Parallel Lives*, p. 39.
13. Keith Howes, 'The media', in *Prejudice and Pride: Discrimination Against Gay People in Modern Britain*, ed. Bruce Galloway (Routledge & Kegan Paul, 1983), p. 200.
14. 'Bona Seances' from *Julian & Sandy*, BBC Radio Collection, BBC Enterprises Ltd, 1992.
15. 'Parlarez-vous? A look at gay slang', *Square Peg*, issue 27, 1990.
16. Burton, *Parallel Lives*, p. 41.
17. Watson, 'Parlare as a second language'.
18. See Bruce Rodgers, *The Queen's Vernacular: A Gay Lexicon* (Blond & Briggs, 1972).
19. Rodgers, introduction to *The Queen's Vernacular*.

Chapter six

A Row of Pink Tents

Call me secretive – It's just between you and me
Call me argumentative – I'm afraid I disagree
Call me into bondage – I'll tie you to the chair
Call me InterFlora – I'll put flowers in my hair
Call me a taxi – and I'll drive you round the bend
Call me a mechanic – and I'll show you my big end

Something strangers noticed
When they peered into my pram
Uncanny and Unnatural
That's what I am.

> Julian Clary, 'Uncanny and unnatural'[1]

ON a cold evening early in 1991, OutRage! – the group that claims it 'puts the camp into campaigning' – held one of their demonstrations outside Bow Street Police Station (infamous for its connections with the trial of Oscar Wilde). The protest aimed to draw attention to gay men's status as 'sex criminals' under the current British laws, and several gay men handed themselves into the police in order to 'confess' to having sexual relationships with other men before reaching the legal age of consent, soliciting in public and procuring. Although not ostensibly camp in intention, Bow Street's setting opposite a prominent opera house induced a fit of queening amongst the couple of hundred protesters, and it wasn't long before shouts of 'We're here, we're queer, we're not going to the opera' resounded along Bow Street. In addition, the appearance of OutRage! 'pretty policemen' dressed in parody uniforms, with feather boas and make-up, created an air of surrealism. When complaining about the OutRage! action to a prominent worker with the opera house, one member of the Metropolitan Police received the abrupt reply that the worker was himself gay and fully supported the action. In addition, he pointed out to the policeman that it was he who was standing on private property, and could he therefore move elsewhere. A disillusioned copper resignedly moved along the pavement.

As the evening progressed, gay men arriving at the opera house and originally intent on attending the opera joined the demonstration outside the police station, causing the police to become more and more anxious. Their officiousness seemed increasingly ridiculous to the (generally peaceful) gathering, and was teasingly sent up and undermined with cat-calls, whistles and shrieks (policemen invariably become the butt of jokes at OutRage! demonstrations, except when they're throwing demonstrators down stairs or loading them into police vans). As senior police officers cursed 'that Peter Tatchell' (organizer of the protest), their outrage both titilated and encouraged the gathered 'sex criminals'. The starry night had already provided a velvet backcloth for the events, but a sudden flurry of snow added an increasingly aesthetic dimension to the final 'confessions' in the police stations. There was a series of standing ovations for the 'sex criminals' as they emerged from the police station. After briefly resurrecting Wilde's spirit in an act of collective dissidence, the assembled queens disappeared either into the night or into the opera house (or the nearest pub) with only a flurry of snowflakes to cover their footsteps.

Although it's not the most renowned example of camp, the Bow Street action illustrates the current marriage between camp and politics, and the conscious reappropriation of camp as a theatrical manoeuvre and an explicitly gay gesture. The more seriously the police reacted to the situation, and the more officiously they attempted to act, the camper the situation became. Defusing or disempowering the police's own authority through camp, camp became more effective as a tool in defining and controlling the meaning and tone of the demonstration. The police were attempting to construct an authority, which then became a target to undermine and parody, at the same time illustrating and exposing the ludicrousness of the laws the demonstration had been targeting. Having already attracted media attention in the campaign, the presence of cameras and radio equipment also created a self-conscious role-play in which the police had to act out their function as guardians of discriminatory law, whilst at the same time being parodied for that very role. The traditionally problematic relationship between camp and politics was bridged by the part played by the police force themselves, who performed as the perfect foils *against* (or on to) which the medium of camp could be focused.

This is all very easy to say, but what is 'camp'? If there's controversy over the very cause of (homo)sexuality, the origins and meaning of camp are equally as problematic. There is little doubt that it can be associated with homosexuality in a general sense, although it is not exclusively homosexual. Homosexuality does not own camp, and not all homosexuals are camp. But – and traditionally this has been a big but – the phrases and characteristics which exemplify camp are often gay. Camp does not simply mean effeminacy, and effeminacy does not necessarily denote camp. It has often been associated with style, although camp itself is not a particular style, but can be recognized in certain styles. It has been associated with a sensibility, but that sensibility has never been defined. It has also been associated with sensitivity, artistry and wit, but is not exclusive to these areas or even necessarily inherent in them.

Camp is often trashy, but not all trash is camp. It has been equated with postmodernism, but is certainly part of other aesthetic or cultural movements and predates many of them. Like Zen, camp is more often defined as that which it is not – a pint of lager is not generally camp, but a pint of lager shandy might be, and if it is drunk through a straw, held in a certain way or poured into a particular glass, it probably would be. Camp is rarely serious, but invariably things will be seriously camp. Camp is certainly nothing new, but it has no history to it, and it is difficult to predict its future. Many of the theatrical manoeuvres already discussed have elements of camp about them, but none of them has an exclusive right to the properties of camp, and none is exclusively camp. Although you can use the phrase 'As camp as a row of pink tents', a row of pink tents is not necessarily camp.

If nothing else, the semantics of camp are always good for a lively discussion. It has enjoyed a certain amount of intellectual respectability, most notably since Susan Sontag analysed it respectfully in her ground-breaking 1964 essay, 'Notes on "camp"'. Sontag's own coda to her notes on the subject is worth further investigation before examining the phenomenon of camp any further: 'the essence of Camp is its love of the unnatural: of artifice and exaggeration. And Camp is esoteric – something of a private code, a badge of identity even, among small urban cliques. . . . To talk about Camp is therefore to betray it'.[2] Sontag then goes on to claim an untenable position of privilege in believing that she is singularly qualified to discuss camp on the grounds that she can claim that she does not wholeheartedly share its sensibility – both assumptions lending themselves to contradiction. Claiming to discuss camp sensibility for her own edification, Sontag hopes not to (but ultimately does) betray camp, as any analysis of it will do. Once you start dissecting the nature of camp, you're left with individual parts and no whole. My own analysis, therefore, can offer no apology or excuse for such a betrayal except that – like camp itself – it is deemed necessary. Sontag's own betrayal strengthened rather than weakened camp as a sensibility, if only because of camp's resolute indifference to her definitions and analysis. For all the intellectual and aesthetic theorizing of camp, it has been neither influenced nor changed by the discourse and is unlikely to be influenced by it in any way in the future.

Contrary to Sontag's opinion, it is my belief that the only people who can offer analysis and coherent discussion (call it betrayal if you will) are those who do share its sensibility, without the level of detachment Sontag claims as her ally. Such distance may not only misrepresent camp, but runs the risk of losing sight of it altogether. Although Sontag's essay is admirable and offers much incisive judgement into camp (and one suspects that she is much more predisposed to camp than her statements allow), much of the importance of her essay is in her perversion and misrepresentation of the subject. In turn, this has misled and misinformed much of the subsequent debate on the subject and led to an overemphasis of discussion of style over content. Sontag asserts that camp is *all* style, an aesthetic phenomenon: 'To emphasize style is to slight content, or to introduce an attitude which is neutral with respect to content. It goes without saying that the Camp sensibility is disengaged, depoliticized – or at least apolitical'.[3]

Sontag's liberalization of camp tradition and her overemphasis on style misreads camp's encoded criticisms, and negates its mercurial energy. Content is an important part of camp, most particularly so when there is the possibility or threat of it being made unimportant. Style in and of itself does not create a camp sensibility, and camp is its own style, precariously balancing meaning with the meaningless. Camp engages and politicizes by providing alternative, even oblique, sensibilities which broaden and more often than not challenge traditional ways of perceiving situations and objects. It creates new ways of seeing and relating to authority. What has been misread in camp is its subversiveness, its use of subterfuge. Camp is always undermining authority, whether this be aesthetic, literary or artistic 'rules' or political or social power. Camp achieves this undermining through its penchant for the incredible, fantastic or fabulous. The chant 'We're here, we're queer, we're fabulous' is a camp testament to the ability to create identity and explore possibilities. Camp invariably has a problematic and implicitly critical relationship with any authority which claims to own power or attempts to define and control a set of ideas, beliefs or aesthetics. Camp has been seen as neutral because it rarely bites the hand that feeds it – it's more likely to nibble. Although camp is not inherently apolitical, this quality is sometimes claimed for it. Camp is pragmatic rather than dogmatic, and what Sontag sees as depoliticization through style, I would see as complication through a splintering of dogmatic viewpoints. Sontag goes some way to noting this facet of camp later on in her essay: 'The whole point of Camp is to dethrone the serious. Camp is playful, anti-serious. More precisely, Camp involves a new, more complex relation to "the serious". One can be serious about the frivolous, frivolous about the serious'.[4]

Although Sontag views camp as neutral, playful and harmless, it is invariably the weapon of the underdog in attempting to defuse or deconstruct the power of authority. To this extent, its power has often been misunderstood or deliberately understated, so that camp's effectiveness has been deliberately disguised within a series of contradictions and self-effacing witticisms. George Melly, in his introduction to Philip Core's menagerie of camp, *Camp: The Lie That Tells the Truth*, illustrates this perfectly:

> That Camp is usually self-mocking is evident, that it signifies arrested emotional development is frequently the case. When camp is tragic, and it can be, it is always personal and never universal. That it is sometimes silly and snobbish is obvious. It is however always, and at whatever cost, a cry against conformity, a shriek against boredom, a testament to the potential uniqueness of each of us and our rights to that uniqueness.[5]

Camp attempts to undermine expectations – of role, identity, perception and restrictions. What Melly sees as self-mockery could perhaps better be characterized as irony. The nature of irony often seen in camp lends itself to various postmodern perceptions of camp, where the target is seen to be authenticity, and camp becomes a form of parody or pastiche. This interpretation has led Jonathan Dollimore to reject the idea of camp as a gay sensibility, on the grounds that 'camp is an invasion and subversion of other sensibilities, and works via parody, pastiche and exaggeration'.[6] Dollimore therefore sees camp as an interpretation of other forms and ideas, sees that it has no form itself. While I can agree with this up to a point, I would suggest that Dollimore overemphasizes camp's reliance on other forms in order to mimic them – camp does not necessarily parody or mimic, but does often contextualize itself in opposition to other ideas. Camp can be applied to the mimicry or parody of other sensibilities but is not wholly defined or generated by them. That is, it does not simply fulfil a dichotomous role in providing a distinct or recognizable 'opposite', but attacks the authority of that idea or form in order to suggest a range of other (fantastic) possibilities. In suggesting this as a way of looking at camp, my emphasis is on camp's creativity and its ability to be obliquely critical (particularly) of the status quo. Camp is therefore invariably about change, acting to suggest forms of departure from those orthodoxies which present themselves as authentic or authoritative.

The fact that camp is often discussed in terms of lists of 'what it is' and 'what it is not' (again originated by Sontag's own discussion of the subject) suggests that camp is neither a quality in and of itself nor simply an opposite or alternative to something else. Camp is outside of itself – neither that which is nor that which is not. A preferred explanation might be that camp is a contextualized array of different, often unlikely (and frequently fabulous) possibilities. The gay artist Philip Core illustrated this in his study of camp in a list of 'Camp rules', some of which are worthy of noting here:

Camp depends on where you pitch it.

Camp is character limited to context.

Camp is in the eyes of the beholder, especially if the beholder is camp.

Camp is not necessarily homosexual. Anyone or anything can be camp. But it takes one to know one.

Camp was a prison for an illegal minority, now it is a holiday for consenting adults.

Camp is first of all a second childhood.

Camp is a biography written by the subject as if it were about another person.

Camp is a disguise that fails.

Camp is an art without artists.[7]

Core's list of 'Camp rules' is reminiscent of Sontag's own list of 'Notes', but is more consciously camp in both form and content. In his own discussion, Core referred to camp as similar to Jean Cocteau's idea of being something that is 'The lie that tells the truth', originally suggested by Cocteau in a set of aphorisms published by *Vanity Fair* in 1922.[8] To this extent, camp can be seen as shedding light on a subject or area from an alternative point of view, often radically or obliquely so. However, camp is not a form of truth, it is merely another way of looking at or presenting something. Camp fails to define anything within its own terms, but contextualizes the realm of possibilities. Core qualifies his own definition of camp with two fundamentals:

There are only two things essential to camp: a secret within the personality which one ironically wishes to conceal and to exploit, and a peculiar way of seeing things, affected by spiritual isolation, but strong enough to impose itself on others through acts or creations.[9]

The difficulty with Core's explanation is that camp is seen as an inner *essence*, a fundamental truth that becomes disguised and/or revealed through and as camp. I think not only that this is too great a claim for camp, but that it disavows a whole range of campery where the object is not to reveal or conceal but simply to *be*. Invariably, camp is as camp does. It is often in the eye of the beholder, but can be noticed or even misread by other observers. Camp's extension of possibilities is more important than camp's own claim to either authenticity or authority. Camp will always undermine its own authority in order to present a continuing series of improbable possibilities. Rather than being the 'lie that tells the truth', camp represents a grey area which can be mistaken for both truth and deception, but is ultimately not aligned to either. Camp's only true allegiance is to mischief.

The history of camp – 'a form of historicism viewed histrionically'[10] – is also problematic and uncertain, although Core's analysis is perhaps one of the better and more honest ones. The difficulty in deciding what camp is becomes even more difficult when looking at the subject historically. Core himself admits that 'the past was a different country; they camped differently there'.[11] More importantly, he acknowledges that camp was a form of coding within a (particularly homosexual) minority, a result and consequence of repression and invisibility. Its early roots in the twentieth century were a humorous, playful disguise that veiled an unyielding resolution to change the rules of containment and lifestyle.

By the time that Susan Sontag came to write about camp in 1964, things had changed somewhat – homosexuality was beginning to be discussed, and camp was seen as the 'acceptable', aesthetic face of homosexuality – it wasn't related to sex or sexuality, but could be recognized as a code for deviance. Particularly, it was associated with effeminacy, exaggeration and the outrageous. These were attributes which could be marketed during the late 1960s and 1970s, when a particular form of camp became popular, particularly associated with 'trashy' music, fashion and art. However, the mainstreaming of camp eventually also caused its decline – camp sensibility became fashionable, and also went out of fashion. Within the gay community, the emerging liberationist politics saw camp as defamatory and stereotypical, distracting from political arguments about inequality. In the long run, this can be seen as assimilationism on the part of homosexual rights campaigners whose emphasis clearly lay not on difference from but on similarity with heterosexuality. The debates about camp in organizations such as the Gay Liberation Front and the Campaign for Homosexual Equality often ditched camp sensibility in favour of 'respectability' so that camp as a form became misrepresented as outrageous publicity, placatory or publicity-seeking rather than radical or problematic. Core himself analysed this: 'Camp, itself evanescent and protean, inevitably has suffered in our exploitative era, from myriad misinterpretations and mutations at the hands of business interests'.[12]

If camp is subversive, it is hard to find a role for it within mainstream or commercial ideologies – what is presented is camp style without content, which is not camp (as a theatrical manoeuvre) at all. Camp needs to react against dominant ideologies in order to fulfil its purpose as presenting a range of fantastic and improbable possibilities. Although fashionable camp – the acceptance of exaggerated style – reached a peak most recently in the 1970s, camp has begun to be refashioned in the 1990s as political camp, partly as a response to its earlier depoliticization. Because camp has appeal, and can be mistaken as uncritical and harmless, it can also be used as a powerful theatrical tool to emphasize and publicize radical opportunities. Camp's edge lies in its collapsing of sense into nonsense, so that it becomes criticism and entertainment and defies traditional binaries of humorous parody and sensible alternative. Camp itself would rarely be so bold as to claim that it could change anything, in terms of political systems, by and of itself. But its use as a tool, a theatrical manoeuvre, is becoming more and more recognized, particularly within the gay community itself. Camp can be used not only to defuse another's authority, it can be used as presentation.

The revived gay rights organizations in Britain – the Stop the Clause 28 campaign, ACT-UP, OutRage!, the Sisters of Perpetual Indulgence – have capitalized on camp as a specifically gay code, with a particularly gay emphasis and meaning. This has also meant broadening the scope for camp, where the mundane is made magnificent. Perhaps this is what Philip Core was alluding to when he wrote, in what George Melly saw as dangerously close to an elegy, that:

> camp will re-emerge. Indefinable, unshakeable, it is the heroism of people not called upon to be heroes. It will find new ways to react both with and against public tastes, it will selfishly and selflessly shriek on, entertaining the self and the spectator in one mad gesture, oblivious of what it is required to do. Camp is always in the future; that is why the present needs it so badly.[13]

Core's faith in camp was well founded, and the context for camp's re-emergence as a vital and necessary code was sown in the harsh realities of the 1980s. The complacent apoliticism of gay identities in the 1970s and early 1980s, and the increased isolation of radical viewpoints by Thatcherite monetarism and morality, led to increasingly desperate measures on both sides of the political divide. Section 28 of the Local Government Act, passed in 1988, saw an unprecedented increase in lesbian and gay activism as central government attempted to regulate local government's use of finances, specifically (in the case of Section 28) in allocating funds for the 'promotion of homosexuality'. For the first time, the government was legislating against *sexuality* and not sexual behaviour, and also explicitly legislating against lesbianism. A high-profile campaign against the legislation included not only mass demonstrations in Manchester and London but smaller targeted actions to break the wall of silence imposed around the Section 28 debate. Banners and graffiti appeared on public buildings and prominent sites, and pink once again became the colour of resistance and defiance. The emergence of pink triangles on statues and buildings signalled guerrilla tactics that culminated in dramatic and spectacular theatrical manoeuvres. But that was not all.

On 2 February 1988, after amendments to the proposed law were defeated in the committee stage in the House of Lords, angry lesbians abseiled down on ropes into the House itself, shouting 'It's our lives you're dealing with'. Making national news, this inspired type of direct action was highlighted again on 23 May when four lesbians interrupted Sue Lawley's television live news broadcast during the BBC's Six O'Clock News. Although dealt with harshly by the presenter herself – having to fight to keep the protesters out of sight, amidst muffled shouts against what was then Clause 28 – the demonstration reached prime-time viewers. These manoeuvres drew criticism both from within the gay community and from outside it, with claims that the way to deal with Section 28 was through more conventional forms of campaigning and lobbying. If such measures are indeed the only way to achieve reform, we await their success with anticipation. However, the political use of camp around Section 28 certainly helped to raise the issue publicly, and vociferously demonstrated that the government could not interfere with people's lives without expecting a backlash. In response to the criticisms emanating from within the community about such assertive demonstrations, Eric Presland, administrator at the time for the Organisation for Lesbian and Gay Action (OLGA), registered his support for the theatricality of the lesbians' cultural intervention:

> People have always done illegal things in the cause of civil rights. They have killed themselves, they have sat down, they have set fire to things, they have smashed statues, they have defaced money. And they have eventually won their arguments. But we just float down from a public gallery in a mock-Gothic fantasy out of William Morris. What style! What elan! And how very camp. What on earth harm did it do to anyone?[14]

Presland's point touches on another argument for the gay political use of camp, which is to dictate the territory on which arguments are fought. Camp helps us to determine the rules of the game, to put forward our own possibilities, which happen to be not a little queer in tone and content. Because camp is so difficult to pinpoint, to understand, its nuances make its recognition reassuring, protective. It moves the goalposts closer to home, it makes a game out of the unbearable and dictates its own ground rules. If camp didn't beat Section 28, it helped to make the fight worthwhile.

During the 1980s, the enormous private and public scale of the HIV/AIDS pandemic affected the gay community in Britain (and continues to do so) in an unprecedented manner. Isolated by state and society and fired by anger and grief, the rise of groups like ACT-UP also saw the use of camp in direct action and 'zaps'. ACT-UP London used camp to illustrate and underline their political campaigning, at one time creating an enormous sheep to represent the apathy of the general British population in the face of the AIDS crisis. (Unfortunately, the sheep itself fell foul to an infamous series of events in camp history – kidnapped by the Sisters of Perpetual Indulgence and decapitated in a fit of camp pique by members of OutRage!, its head was stuck on a pole and left in the shared ACT-UP/OutRage! office at the London Lesbian and Gay Centre in Farringdon.) ACT-UP's theatrical manoeuvres make deliberate use of camp to effect debate and criticism and are a reflection on and reaction against the horrors of the AIDS crisis over the past decade.

OutRage! have consistently used camp as a theatrical manoeuvre since their inception on 10 May 1990 as a direct action group aimed at fighting homophobia. Most often using camp as a means to an end, they have also occasionally used it as an end in itself. Inspired by a sub-group from the American direct action group Queer Nation, Work It Girl (WIG) was formed as an OutRage! sub-group to 'claim queer space' by shopping in 'urban drag' (frocks, slap and wigs) in the centre of London. The group raised eyebrows as they minced in drag into all their favourite shops to check out the latest bargains, and to proclaim gay visibility. Although the action was decidedly frivolous in character, and certainly did not change the world, it was a camp extravaganza that did no real harm, and lightened an otherwise dull day's shopping. The nature of OutRage!'s direct action often aims to challenge and confront the law, and camp helps to disguise the actual point at which the law is broken – it deceives authority into playfulness and blurs the boundaries between truth and fiction. It has proved itself a useful tool, particularly in goading the media and press into covering actions and debates concerning gay issues. OutRage!'s great success has been in imaginative actions which raise awareness around specific campaigns and actions.

The re-emergence of camp as a useful political weapon and theatrical manoeuvre underlines camp's potential for subversion. It is becoming increasingly associated and aligned with gay identity, after a popular flirtation with commercial exploitation. Camp's ability to survive represents its necessity to gay identity, despite those who deride or deny it as a characteristic or sensibility. Camp will continue to be useful for the foreseeable future, bringing with it not only glamour and fun but criticism and constructive (im)possibilities. Although Susan Sontag might argue that to discuss camp is to betray it, the real betrayal of camp is in defining (and therefore destroying it), limiting it to static categorization and denying its own mischief. Camp is the natural enemy of order and dogma, teasing and flirting with chaotic imaginations. Essentially harmless in character and application, it nevertheless terrifies those wishing to rule or control through dogma. In this sense, (homo)sexual identity as a performative identity, a sense of playfulness in and out of (hetero)sexual definition, structure and category, does have a close alliance with camp sensibility. Camp represents the state of play which denial of compulsory heterosexuality entails, a subversion of traditional and restrictive (unimaginative) conventions. To paraphrase the old idiom, as long as there's Christmas, there'll always be camp.

Notes

1.   Julian Clary, 'Uncanny and unnatural' (Clary/Jungr/Parker). Published by Copyright Control © 1990 Wonderdog Records Ltd.
2.   Susan Sontag, 'Notes on camp', in *A Susan Sontag Reader* (Harmondsworth: Penguin, 1985), p. 105.
3.   Sontag, 'Notes on camp', no. 2. p. 107.
4.   Sontag, 'Notes on camp', no. 41, p. 116.
5.   George Melly, preface to Philip Core, *Camp: The Lie That Tells the Truth* (Plexus, 1984).
6.   Jonathan Dollimore, *Sexual Dissidence* (Oxford: Oxford University Press, 1991), p. 311.

7.   Core, 'Camp rules', in *Camp*.
8.   Core, introduction to *Camp*, p. 9.
9.   Core, introduction to *Camp*, p. 9.
10. Core, 'Camp rules', in *Camp*.
11. Core, introduction to *Camp*, p. 13.
12. Core, introduction to *Camp*, p. 13.
13. Core, introduction to *Camp*, p. 15.
14. Eric Presland, letter to *Gay Times*, March 1988, cited in Stephen Jeffrey-Poulter, *Peers, Queers and Commons* (Routledge, 1991), p. 252.

Part Three
Space

Chapter seven

Giving Birth to Pigs

Neither a lover of the carnival
Amazed that crowds might sway in unison
Nor him who stands at the rear of the church
Drawing solitariness into the injured lung
I pick the public place to be unpublic in
And the sun which brings you rushing
To a nakedness brings bruising to my skin

> Howard Barker, Gary Upright[1]

In the way of the western world
*   the fairies' dance has become small*
* a bleating, crabbed jerkiness*
but there for all that,
*   a bit of healthy green in the dead wood*
*   that spreads an invisible green fire*
*   around and around the globe*
encircling it in its dance
*   of intimacy with the secret of all living things*

> Michael Rumaker, 'The fairies are dancing
> all over the world'[2]

Should we be making oppositional statements in the same
measured, if squeaky voice, or should we be reinventing,
rediscovering theatre with a glorious five-octave range?

> John McGrath, The Bone Won't Break[3]

IN *Epistemology of the Closet*, Eve Kosofsky Sedgwick examines the binary structures caused and defined by the creation of homo- and heterosexualities from the late nineteenth century onwards. Her argument is that in creating homo/heterosexualities, other dualistic concepts have been created which rely on the oppositional categories of sexuality to help maintain them and give them coherence. In addition, categories are so constructed as to rely on their minoritized opposite to define and reassert the dominant selves as powerful – so heterosexuality, crucially, relies on homosexuality to define and create itself. Kosofsky Sedgwick's analysis goes further:

> the now chronic modern crisis of homo/heterosexual definition has affected our culture through its ineffaceable marking particularly of the categories secrecy/disclosure, knowledge/ignorance, private/public, masculine/feminine, majority/minority, innocence/initiation, natural/artificial, new/old, discipline/terrorism, canonic/noncanonic, wholeness/decadence, urbane/provincial, domestic/foreign, health/illness, same/different, active/passive, in/out, cognition/paranoia, art/kitsch, utopia/apocalypse, sincerity/sentimentality, and voluntarity/addiction.[4]

Sedgwick's detailed analysis is of particular interest here because of its discussion of the binary structures attached to the public/private spheres, and of spaces attached to and around the 'closet' of homosexuality and gay identity. How and where gay men present, assert and/or disguise their sexuality has necessarily been the subject of political debate about gay identity and civil rights, conflating the 'private' with the 'political' in an attempt to create public debate, concern and action. At first restricted to manoeuvres carried out largely in secret, after the Second World War the discussion in Britain focused on claiming private space for homosexual acts, and most recently has become centred on the public role and definition of gay identity and community. Space – where sexual identity is revealed and/or celebrated – has largely dictated how sexual identity has been constructed, how it has manifested itself and what theatrical manoeuvres are appropriate (even inappropriate) in creating, defending or deconstructing that space. Although there hasn't been a strictly linear movement from theatrical manoeuvres created around the private (or secret) sphere to the public, there has been a general trend towards public display and spectacle, which reflects the general social and political discourses around sexuality and sexual identity in modern Britain.

Space and expectations concerning public duty or role have been integral to the direction of gay theatrical manoeuvres, and helped to dictate both form and content – the molly houses of eighteenth-century London were secret clubs for homosexuals to meet and carry out rituals which helped to assert and redefine their space and identity. More recently, the theatrical manoeuvres of groups like OutRage! have been upfront and confrontational, asserting a positive gay identity and claiming queer space in all manner of public discourse and activity. The increased visibility and discussion (not to mention consumer buying power) of gay identity/identities has led to a concerted use of theatricality to create and validate new rituals appropriate to the modern gay community, acting as both critique and mirror image of traditional heterosexual celebrations and events.

And so queer weddings, blessings, exorcisms, carnivals, Christmas and Valentine celebrations have all become powerful performances reflecting a confident and assertive gay community aiming to affirm identity through interactive action and events located in the public sphere. The tactics may not be without fault themselves. The historical reclamation of space that began with a hidden subculture now attempts not only to encroach on heterosexually defined events and places but also to create and guard homo-supremacist spaces under the guise of 'queer turf'. Alternatively, assimilation dictates the slavish mimicry of dominant cultural norms. The romantic figurehead of sentimental family entertainment, Cilla Black's television show *Blind Date* (by its own definition exclusively heterosexual), is constantly aped and 'perverted' in gay clubs and pubs across the country, as is the equally heterosexual television version of *Mr and Mrs*. A patchwork of staged events and rituals which merely reflects the exclusivity of heterosexuality hampers the imaginative use of space to redefine – more importantly to deconstruct – artificial boundaries based on mutually exclusive but interdependent notions of sexuality and sexual identity. If the use of space is important to the context and efficacy of theatrical manoeuvres (and I am claiming that it is), then how space and 'territory' can be reconstituted becomes a priority for imagining and creating alternative playgrounds.

The use of space also has political imperatives: when sexual identity is limited to and defined solely by private acts, its regulation can be enforced by private and public censure – a place for everything and everything in its place. The fetishization of private sexuality has subordinated homosexuality to heterosexuality so that public celebrations of sexuality are singularly heterosexual, leaving homosexuality (as it were) in the closet. The result of this is the disenfranchisement of the collective homosexual body or community which – without many of the traditional ties of a biological family – fractures into its several parts come closing time, or the locking of public toilets and parks. The growth of helplines, pubs, clubs and community centres during the 1970s reimagined gay spaces to include non-sexual contact rather than simply fetishizing the genital act, or – in the case of privileged heterosexual 'gentlemen's' clubs – totally excluding them.

The use of the closet as an imaginary space – coming out or staying in – has led to tactical 'outing' of prominent closeted homosexuals in America and (almost) in Britain, prevented only by strict libel laws and prominent (expensive) libel cases in connection with outing campaigns such as that of the Australian soap star and singer Jason Donovan. Outing has brought into question the very idea of 'privacy' – whether in fact sexuality and sexual identity have a place in such a notion, and who has the right to own or name that sexual identity. In questioning how the space of the 'closet' is structured and created, the destructive elements which help to serve heterosupremacy can be exposed and to some extent disarmed.

If drama is the most public of all art forms, it is also the one that may teach us most about our public and private roles as a gay community, and how to reimagine personal and political spaces in rehearsing and recreating new challenges and possibilities. By acting out these alternatives, we can devise tactics and strategies to help us make them real. The following theatrical manoeuvres are examined as performances of one kind or another, looking in particular at the different use of space in each case and the varied ways in which (historically) theatricality and ritual have been employed by the gay community.

The impertinent decorum of molly houses

The growth of 'molly houses' in urban London during the early eighteenth century provided opportunities for homosexuals to meet in secret for sex and company. A number of such clubs later developed and were the beginnings of an elaborate gay subculture that protected and nourished its members. The molly houses existed before homosexuality was medically and socially defined as an identity rather than as a sodomitical (unnatural) act, and can be seen perhaps as one of the nascent points of a homosexual subculture. Infamous in their day, the molly houses were often the object of police raids and obvious targets for moral crusading agencies such as the Societies for the Reformation of Manners. Less public than the open cruising grounds, they afforded some protection and privacy for homosexual encounters and a base from which to build up a network of friendships and liaisons while allowing their regulars to continue their everyday lives. As Alan Bray has pointed out, their purpose was not solely for procuring sexual partners:

> Surrounded as the molly houses were by intense disapproval and at least partly hidden, they must have seemed like any ghetto, at times claustrophobic and oppressive, at others warm and reassuring. It was a place to take off the mask. It is as much in such terms as in actual sexual encounters that we should now envisage what a molly house was like.[5]

The molly houses, or 'mollying culls' as they became known in Parlyaree, were often part of a tavern, where alcohol, singing and dancing were freely available. If the meeting was not in a tavern, drink was brought into somebody's house and sold to the customers, who could number as many as fifty on a busy night. There would be dancing, singing and bawdiness, with men dressed in women's clothes and acting effeminately, calling each other such names as Miss Fanny Knight, Pomegranate Molly, Dip-Candle Mary or Princess Seraphina. As Rictor Norton has recorded in *Mother Clap's Molly House*, such names were often 'suggested by a wide range of physiognomic characteristics, occupational status, geographical origins and personality traits', although such 'maiden names' indicated neither the part played in gender role-play nor necessarily occupation or employment.[6] They were rather part of the elaborate culture of the molly houses, as Randolph Trumbach has noted in his essay *The Birth of the Queen*:

> even the men who were married to women adopted female names once inside the molly house. It had become the case that after 1700 most adult sodomites were both active and passive, whereas before 1700 only a minority of sodomites had been so.[7]

Moreover, within the confines of the molly house, behaviour was generally uninhibited, from both the effects of alcohol and general good will. Samuel Stevens's account at the trial of Margaret Clap (one of the more famous molly house owners) in 1725 indicates:

> I found between 40 and 50 men making love to one another, as they called it. Sometimes they would sit in one another's laps, kissing in a lewd manner and using their hands indecently. Then they would get up, dance and make curtsies, and mimic the voices of women . . . then they would hug, and play, and toy, and go out by couples into another room on the same floor to be married, as they called it.[8]

Sometimes a molly house would hold a ball or masquerade when elaborate and beautiful costumes might be worn. The accounts indicate that the mollies created easily accessible but secret meeting houses and rooms, which became 'playgrounds' for an emerging (homo)sexual identity, significantly different from homosexual (or sodomitical) encounters in the previous century. Part of this emergent identity (or alternative identity) was the ritualization of ceremonies and friendships which took place in the molly houses, often using and subverting socially acceptable forms and institutions such as marriage. The molly houses became not only a meeting place for mollies but a distinct culture with rules and rituals of their own in an unprecedented way. Two of the most significant ceremonies appear to be the molly marriages and birthing rituals, which can be seen as significant forms of early theatrical manoeuvres.

'Marrying' rituals were an important part of molly house life during the eighteenth century, and became infamous themselves in subsequent trials and court cases. Although the marriages themselves never seemed intended to be permanent, or even particularly serious affairs, they were of consequence in ritualizing molly relationships and social relations. Light-hearted in tone and form, they remain somewhat mysterious, with only a few glimpses of how they might have been conducted. We do know that within the molly house, there was a room referred to often as the 'chapel' or 'marrying room', where couples were married on a wedding night. Although the mollies often used their 'maiden names' when talking to and about each other, partners were always referred to as husbands rather than wives, with endearments such as 'special sweetheart'. Although it is not recorded who celebrated the weddings, it is unlikely to have been a conventional minister, although a molly marriage of 1728 records the presence of stewards, and presumably some ceremonial head figure would have been present to conduct the ceremonies.[9]

The marriages seem to have been a rite of passage to attain access to the bedroom, or chapel, rather than a formal and permanent commitment or straightforward copy of the heterosexual legal, social and religious institution. The wedding may have been a formalization of the two men's intention to have sex, but was rarely expected to mark a single and lifelong commitment in the way that heterosexual marriages do. This is not to say that there weren't long-lasting relationships between mollies, and instances of deep relationships and friendships can be found. The 'molly marriage', however, seems to have served a very different and particular function to conventional marriages, and does not seem to have had the same meaning even for those mollies who were actually married to women. The references to marrying and chapels indicate a formalization of a self-conscious homosexual – or molly – identity, and one which used and welcomed the ritualization and socialization of (homo)sexuality. As Alan Bray has pointed out:

> [the normalization of homosexuality] was achieved by means of their own society, both in the sense that within them homosexuality was no longer perverse as it was elsewhere, but also in that homosexuality quite objectively was the organising point around which its whole culture – its way of life, its manners, its behaviour – was built; within molly houses it was given a significance in direct proportion to its rejection elsewhere.[10]

Although it's difficult to assess the performance value of molly marriages as they are not recorded in detail, we can see them as semi-public ceremonies, conducted in the private but infamous molly houses of the time. To this extent, there was access to the events, and participation in them was social rather than exclusively private.

The molly marriages also bring into question the role of performative gender and sexual identities, and how they changed according to where they were (allowed to be) presented. Outside the security of the molly house, molly marriages are almost unthinkable, and perhaps the structure of the space and ceremony themselves reflect the pressures and strictures of outside organizations. The idea of formal homosexual marriage has led Marjorie Garber to comment that:

> the pleasures – and the sometimes deconstructive, sometimes assimilationist effects – of playing with patriarchal structures is nowhere more in evidence than in the conjunction of homosexuality, transvestism, and that cornerstone of normatively heterosexual institutions: marriage. For it is in the discussion of 'marriage' that the necessary questioning of the idea of the 'original' and the 'copy' has taken its most effective form.[11]

In making this assertion, Garber analyses the continuing tradition of male-only marriages, most particularly in the western world where its relationship to the traditional heterosexual wedding is most pronounced and striking. Garber tentatively suggests that 'in a way, all marriages, even heterosexual marriages, are "mock marriages" in their dependence upon certain aspects of sartorial tradition and ceremony', particularly the elaborate bridal gown.[12] With particular relevance to the molly marriages of the early eighteenth century, Garber cites Judith Butler's contention from *Gender Trouble* that heterosexuality and homosexuality are neither copy nor original but necessary opposites reliant on each other for their existence in a discourse about sexuality: 'The repetition of heterosexual constructs within sexual cultures both gay and straight may well be the inevitable site of the denaturalization and mobilization of gender categories'.[13] Perhaps, then, molly marriages do not so much represent a mere copy of heterosexual marriage as fulfil a need in and of themselves, partly modelled on existing (outside) institutions, yet also involving peculiarly molly traditions and rituals?

In her controversial modern gay and lesbian prayer book, *Daring to Speak Love's Name*, Dr Elizabeth Stuart elucidates her feelings on gay 'friendships' as worthy of ceremony and celebration:

> 'Friendship' suggests a relationship of equals who delight in each other's company and have concern for each other's well-being. 'Friendship' also conjures up images of inclusivity rather than exclusivity. Most of our important relationships can be described as 'friendships' and so our most important relationship becomes part of the network of friendship which sustains and nourishes us. The concept of friendship also admits diversity, and lesbian and gay relationships are nothing if not diverse.[14]

Whilst not wishing clumsily to impose our own modern concepts on historical situations, we could usefully apply Stuart's comments to the emerging molly culture, and may go some way in helping to explain the role and significance of 'molly marriages'. It may be that they ritualized the (sexual) union of two husbands in a manner which could be understood and accepted by those within the molly house, using conventional marriage ceremonies as the foundation with which to explore and celebrate male sexual and social relationships with men. In developing alternative identities and rituals, the mollies may have been exercising implicit criticisms of their society in a protected but accessible environment. Indeed, Alan Bray has pointed to the problematic existence of what seems to be a contradictory but nevertheless planned authoritarian response to the existence of the molly houses. Short-lived but high-profile police raids on the molly houses seemed to be moral exercises intended not to put an end to the molly houses as such, but to curtail their growth. Bray goes on to suggest that the molly houses themselves also had a public role in that they allowed mollies to meet surreptitiously in private, while at the same time limiting and controlling how and where those meetings might take place: 'they served, in effect a dual purpose, for they must have restricted the spread of homosexuality at the same time as they secured its presence'.[15]

The marriage ceremonies were part of securing a molly identity, and were only one of a series of ceremonies that the mollies conducted or took part in. More controversial and outrageous were the 'mock births' which also took place within the confines of the molly houses and which have been referred to in court trials of the period. The births or 'Lying-ins' involved a molly dressing as in female attire and 'giving birth' to a jointed wooden doll or even a whole cheese, with attendants to help and christen the 'baby'. Rictor Norton records Ned Ward's contemporaneous account of the ceremony:

Not long since[,] they cushioned up one of their Brethren, or rather Sisters, according to Female Dialect, disguising him in a Woman's Night-Gown, Sarsanet Hood, & Night-rail[,] who when the Company were men, was to mimick a woman, produce a jointed Baby they had provided, which wooden Offspring was to be afterwards Christened, whilst one in a High Crown'd Hat, I am [t]old old Bedlam's Pinner, representing a Country Midwife, & another dizen'd up in a

Huswife's Coif for a Nurse & all the rest of an impertinent decorum of a Christening.[16]

The account naturally raises interest in what might have happened afterwards. Was the baby 'named'? Did the doll itself become significant or important in the life of the molly house? Was it retained by the 'mother'? Did anybody dare claim to be the 'father' in such a ceremony? How often would a ceremony of this nature take place? In his own assessment of the mock births, Norton resists the temptation to see them simply as mimicry or parody, and suggests connections with tribal ceremonies in New Guinea and amongst Mohave Indians, who perform similar 'birthing' rituals in order to exorcize evil spirits or sickness. Norton also cites a ceremony in King James I's bedchamber, where the Duchess of Buckingham gave 'birth' to a pig, ostensibly to amuse the ailing king. Norton concludes that:

> The mollies were under daily pressures from a hostile society not to express their emotions, or run the risk of being hanged or publicly shamed in the pillory. Occasional 'lyings-in' could serve to relieve their collective anxiety through outrageous fun, and what today is called 'camp' behaviour.[17]

What the purpose of the lying-ins was is difficult to tell, although Norton's analysis highlights their ceremonial aspect, and there is little doubt that given the pressures of early eighteenth-century moral reformers, the safety of the molly house did provide opportunity and cause for celebration and revelry. Whether the focus of the wooden doll was indeed as complex as Norton suggests seems doubtful, requiring a degree of sophistication and political critique that is not in evidence elsewhere in the molly culture. This sort of ritual could have meant almost anything, from being a fertility (virility) ceremony to mirroring or marking actual births connected with the molly or events connected with the molly culture, although all such theories are merely conjecture. What is important is that they were treated as events – costumes were used, and people took on roles in the celebration. They were mini-performances, given to the molly club, involving props and active participation. There seems to be a sense of fun or what Ward intriguingly labels 'impertinent decorum' about the proceedings.

Not only, then, were the mollies developing a theatrical identity – acting out an alternative identity based on their homosexuality – but they were also developing rituals and occasions with which to celebrate that identity. The homosexual 'subculture' was developing from being concerned only with sexual liaisons towards creating a coherent network of places and events where homosexual identity could be shared, demonstrated and celebrated. Central to this was the need for the relatively safe space of the molly house itself, which provided the structure for meetings and rituals.

The molly houses were visible and well enough known for people searching them out to find them. They were also private enough – unless there was a sudden raid – for customers to be allowed relative discretion in their affairs. Further, given the nature of the molly houses themselves, it is likely that attitudes within them towards ceremonies such as the molly marriages and lying-ins would have been supportive and appreciative of the cultural (re)inventions and encouraging of deviant or impertinent creativity. The grotesque theatricality of the rituals is reminiscent of the pantomime tradition, and so perhaps we might see in them early relatives of the modern panto Dame, and some of the British pantomimic slapstick that proves so popular today. The ceremonies and rituals are, as Norton's account of the James I 'pig-birth' indicates, similar to court masquerades of the time and reveal a lively and irreverent interest in spectacle and popular forms of entertainment. Faced with the threat of exposure and possible suicide as a result, the molly house rituals reflected both daring and knowing caution in the personality of the participants, both sides of the coin having their own particular allure.

Frustrating though it is not to have more information about the weddings and lying-ins, they do fit in with a long pattern of gay reworkings of conventional (heterosexual) communal ceremonies. As Norton points to 'birthing' ceremonies in different cultures, Garber in *Vested Interests* also discusses transvestite or cross-dressing male–male marriages, and certainly modern interest in 'queer weddings' was highlighted by OutRage! in Trafalgar Square in June 1991 with a mass queer wedding, when same-sex couples plighted their troth and a year later attempted to become legally married in registry offices.

Although having different significance in different cultures, the act of celebrating such events as these unions seems almost commonplace, and it is in the variety and difference between such ceremonies, as well as in their similarities, that the breadth of gay theatrical manoeuvres is revealed. One of the major developments we can see in the strategy of ceremonial manoeuvres is their movement from private or secret locations into the public arena, where homosexuality becomes not only a cause for celebration but also confrontation, treating gay identity not as a secret shared but a sexuality exposed. Even before the Stonewall riots of 1969, as early as 1698, Captain Rigby was asserting a form of gay pride before being entrapped by a young man, William Minton, in St James's Park, as his trial records:

> then to incite Minton thereto spake blasphemous words and further said that the French King did it and the Czar of Muscovy made Alexander, a carpenter, a prince for that purpose and affirmed he had seen the Czar of Muscovy through a hole at sea lie with Prince Alexander.[18]

A self-conscious sense of community history around (homo)sexuality is ordinarily attributed to the liberation movements of the twentieth century, but in adopting traditions and ceremonies which were communal in nature and which emphasized continuing relationships and/or community, the molly house culture was acknowledging its own historicity and possible futures. Birthing and marrying – associated ordinarily with the continuation or procreation of existence – may indeed have been attempts to preserve or encourage communal identities and networks. Elizabeth Stuart's emphasis on friendship and allegiances reveals the vulnerability of sexual identities. They are essentially social, and need social events or occasions to give them meanings.

Ceremonies also helped to create, define and bless the space of the molly house itself. Not only drinking, dancing and intimacy took place: the club members could initiate rights and rituals which gave them a sense of belonging and particularly a group identity. An unpublic place to be public in, it created a clandestine space in which a conventionally public spectacle or affirmation of loyalty or continuance might be acknowledged.

Notes

1. Howard Barker, *Gary Upright*, in *Gary the Thief/Gary Upright* (John Calder, 1987), pp. 34–5.
2. Michael Rumaker, 'The fairies are dancing all over the world', in *The Penguin Book of Homosexual Verse*, ed. Stephen Coote (Harmondsworth: Penguin, 1983), pp. 396–7.
3. John McGrath, *The Bone Won't Break: On Theatre and Hope in Hard Times* (Methuen, 1990), p. 155.
4. Eve Kosofsky Sedgwick, *Epistemology of the Closet* (Brighton: Harvester Wheatsheaf, 1991), p. 11.
5. Alan Bray, *Homosexuality in Renaissance England* (GMP, 1982), p. 84.
6. Rictor Norton, *Mother Clap's Molly House: The Gay Subculture in England 1700–1830* (GMP, 1991), pp. 92–6.
7. Randolph Trumbach, 'The birth of the queen: sodomy and the emergence of gender equality in modern culture, 1660–1750', in *Hidden from History: Reclaiming the Gay & Lesbian Past*, ed. Martin Bauml Duberman, Martha Vicinus and George Chauncey, Jr (New York: New American Library, 1989), p. 139.
8. *Select Trials*, vol. 3, p. 37, cited in Bray, *Homosexuality in Renaissance England*, p. 81.
9. Norton, *Mother Clap's Molly House*, pp. 100–1.
10. Bray, *Homosexuality in Renaissance England*, pp. 98–9.
11. Marjorie Garber, *Vested Interests: Cross-Dressing & Cultural Anxiety* (Routledge, 1992).
12. Garber, *Vested Interests*, p. 142.
13. Judith Butler, *Gender Trouble: Feminism and the Subversion of Identity* (Routledge, 1990), p. 31.
14. Dr Elizabeth Stuart, *Daring to Speak Love's Name – A Gay and Lesbian Prayer Book* (Hamish Hamilton, 1992), p. 19.
15. Bray, *Homosexuality in Renaissance England*, p. 102.
16. Edward Ward, 'The history of the London clubs' (London, 1709), p. 29, cited in Norton, *Mother Clap's Molly House*, p. 98.
17. Norton, *Mother Clap's Molly House*, p. 99.
18. *Compleat Collection of Remarkable Tryals*, vol. 1, p. 239, cited in Bray, *Homosexuality in Renaissance England*, p. 98.

Chapter eight

Rupert Bear Meets Some Radical Fairies

Actor/Drag Queen: *And the story continues.*
In the Middle Ages they burned witches. Witches were
usually women who lived without men.
So they burned the lesbians; and when doing so, they
tied together in bundles men who loved each other, to
kindle the fire at the feet of the women.
These were the faggots. And the story continues.
Until the riots in Christopher Street, gay men had
forgotten that their burning bodies had provided a torch
to consume the women. No one bothered to remind
them. Their attempts and their failures had ignored that.
When the men finally emerged from the bars, and onto
the streets of New York, they found that the women
were up there as well.
And our stories continue.

Noel Greig and Drew Griffiths, As Time Goes By[1]

ON 27 June 1969, Judy Garland was buried. An estimated
22,000 people paid their respects to the funeral home. Later that
night, at nearly 2 o'clock in the morning, the Manhattan police
attempted a raid on a gay bar, the Stonewall Inn, in Greenwich
Village, New York. Although raids on gay bars were not uncom-
mon, this particular raid made history. As a crowd gathered out-

side, and customers were taken away to waiting police vans, violence erupted in the bar itself:

> the scene became explosive. Limp wrists were forgotten. Beer cans and bottles were heaved at the windows and a rain of coins descended on the cops. . . . Almost by signal the crowd erupted into cobblestone and bottle heaving. . . . From nowhere came an uprooted parking meter – used as a battering ram on the Stonewall door. I heard several cries of 'let's get some gas', but the blaze of flame which soon appeared in the window of Stonewall was still a shock.[2]

The rioting that night lasted forty-five minutes, and was repeated throughout the weekend. Graffiti appeared proclaiming 'Gay Power', and the Stonewall riots set the tone for a new era of gay militancy and consciousness which quickly gathered roots during the last months of the 'Swinging Sixties' and into the new decade of the 1970s. The Stonewall riots firmly brought homosexuality into the public arena and violently repudiated the myth that homosexuals were unable or unwilling to defend or assert their civil rights.

The New York Gay Liberation Front was formed as a result of the Stonewall riots, and was a much more aggressive organization than its 'homophile' counterpart, the Mattachine Society. Its message was not only that 'gay is good' but that gay men and lesbians should have pride in their sexuality, and that gay liberation was part of the civil rights movement, and on a par with equal rights campaigns for blacks and women. It was a revolutionary organization which saw homosexuality as a political issue, and therefore one which was not simply confined to private acts but connected to public and societal identity. In Britain, the Gay Liberation Front was started in London in the autumn of 1970. It was founded by Aubrey Walter and Bob Mellors, two gay men who had met in America, and although the first meeting at the London School of Economics attracted only nineteen people, the GLF eventually began drawing four to five hundred to its public meetings. The GLF produced leaflets and newsletters, held workshops, meetings, discos and political 'zaps' or demonstrations. Much more radical than the Committee for Homosexual Equality (later to become the Campaign for Homosexual Equality), it grew very quickly, and ultimately collapsed in almost as short a period.

The GLF's manifesto highlighted the importance of 'coming out', of being open about (homo)sexuality and being visibly proud of it. The first and most obvious stage of this was to announce it to friends, family, workmates. They saw the 'personal as political' and the closet as one of the main instruments of heterosexist oppression. Flamboyant and confrontational, GLF summed up the mood of a new generation in Britain who had seen the partial decriminalization of homosexuality and were now demanding much more. Strongly influenced by leftist politics, the GLF also saw themselves as building alliances with other oppressed minorities and viewed gay liberation as fitting in with a much broader agenda of (radical) social change.

The GLF's first demonstration was a torchlit procession across Highbury Fields on 27 November 1970 to protest against the arrest of Louis Eakes, a Young Liberal leader, for alleged 'importuning'. Almost two hundred people gathered together and demonstrated gay pride, openly kissing and linking arms. The demonstration was the first of many, which eventually became more and more theatrical as the street theatre group organized such zaps as that outside the Miss World contest in 1970, holding an alternative 'Miss-Used' competition outside the Albert Hall (where tomatoes to throw were supplied by local market stalls).

The most spectacular 'zap' occurred in September 1971, at the theatrical launch of the Festival of Light, a right-wing campaign against pornography and obscenity, largely organized by self-proclaimed 'moral reformer' Mrs Mary Whitehouse. The Festival of Light was inspired by Peter Hill who, on returning to England after spending four years in India, asked God for three signs that He favoured such a project, which he apparently received. A grand rally was organized at London's Central Hall, attracting a large collection of celebrities, fundamentalist Christians and moralists, including speakers such as Cliff Richard, Malcolm Muggeridge and Mary Whitehouse herself. Set up as an exclusive public meeting, for which tickets were issued, the Festival of Light was planning to recruit members and interest as part of an ongoing national campaign. The September rally was promoted as a grand occasion, a performance in itself – which is exactly what it turned out to be.

Having obtained tickets and programmes through an infiltration of the Festival's steering committee, GLF demonstrators gathered together at Westminster Bridge to launch a counter-demonstration which went under the umbrella title of 'Operation Rupert'. The name referred to the prosecution of the underground magazine *Oz* and specifically its publication the *Little Red School Book*, which featured an alternative 'Rupert Bear' cartoon strip. Indeed, Operation Rupert itself was later reported in a truly fantastic form by the GLF themselves in *Come Together 10*, in the parody cartoon strip 'Rupert Bear and the other people':

> One day Rupert Bear invited all his forest friends to do a street theatre. They were all very excited and met him at Covent Garden, dressed in their best clothes. There was Jesus with his toy cross, the Bible-reading priest, Mrs Mary Whitehouse, a choir singing 'All Things Bright and Beautiful', some jolly policemen with red noses and cans of CS gas. . . . there was also a very pretty little fairy called the Spirit of Porn, and some schoolteachers with canes and five nuns.[3]

Operation Rupert was engineered as a series of co-ordinated stunts, each of which took its cue from the preceding action. None of the participants knew the whole plan, only the cue for their particular act. Dressed specially for the occasion, it was even difficult to distinguish other GLF members from 'genuine' members of the Festival of Light. As the ceremonies began, with a series of speeches and testimonies by international dignitaries on the platform, the hall resounded with delighted applause at the end of each speech. As the speeches wore on, so did the clapping, becoming longer, louder and slower every time. This was the first phase of the protest, eventually resulting in the disruptive members of the gathering being hastily removed by stewards. A youth group began shouting from the balcony and disrupting speakers. As a Dane stood up to deplore the evils of pornography, the level of protest took a dramatic turn:

Now pandemonium broke loose . . . Mice were released. Stink bombs were thrown. Bubbles were blown by a pretty girl in a girl-guide uniform. The Dane gave up, and for the first time the choir was wheeled in as a way of crushing protest: the red ranks rose and sang us to perdition. A banner went up proclaiming 'Cliff for Queen'.[4]

The mice (provided by Graham Chapman from *Monty Python*) were joined by a flutter of released butterflies, and after she had been punched in the back, the girl guide tipped her bubble liquid over the balcony on to the hats of the women below. The stewards reacted quickly, if violently, and warned a group of nuns to pray for the souls of the demonstrators. The nuns took to the stage and danced, being none other than at least one man and several lesbians from the GLF. The mice began climbing up the furs of women in the audience and Bette Bourne, dressed as an English gentleman, loudly complained about being violently manhandled, accusing a woman in front of him of having violence in her eyes. After having being prepared at the back of the hall while pretending to suffer a fainting fit, drag queen Michael James burst down the aisle as a Southern Belle in a beige frock (with full circle skirt and pearl buttons), proclaiming at the top of his voice that he'd been saved. A bemused Malcolm Muggeridge announced from the platform that he didn't like homosexuals. Men kissing in the foyer were extricated as police were called, one policeman later being so surprised by a kiss on the cheek that he fell backwards and his helmet dropped off.

After the protest, two organizers from the Festival of Light condescended to allowing four protesters to voice their objections to the rally inside the hall, and some members of the audience later took the opportunity to talk to the demonstrators outside the rally. Operation Rupert made the national papers that week and overshadowed the festival itself. Later, in September of that year, an alternative 'Festival of Light' meeting was held in Hyde Park, which the GLF attended in order to demonstrate their ongoing concern with the anti-Festival-of-Light movement.

Operation Rupert represents one of the most daring and well-directed theatrical manoeuvres of the early gay liberation movement in Britain. Its political success lies in its focus – a select group of conservative moral campaigners who defined themselves as representative of the British public and self-appointed guardians against corruption and obscenity. Operation Rupert disrupted the very heart of its activity, infiltrating both its steering committee and the most important event of its campaign. It showed that there were other groups equally (if not more) organized and capable of rallying support and attracting media attention. It also succeeded in puncturing the over-inflated egos of those involved in the Festival of Light – if the Festival could not prevent infiltration, and by extension corruption, of its own house, how could it possibly claim to protect and represent Britain as a whole? Their authority had been severely challenged and eventually undermined, not simply in terms of ideas but also in terms of style and presentation.

The Festival of Light was itself a performance, presented in the prestigious Central Hall, and with star performers such as Cliff Richard and Malcolm Muggeridge. The cast presented themselves as concerned Christians, dressed in their 'Sunday best', parts they had been taught to play by institutions such as the Church, roles that fitted completely into the Festival's philosophy. Their own capacity to adopt new roles and change behaviour was acknowledged as an important part of the Festival itself, with testimonies of how God had changed their lives, and made them into different people. Although presented as genuine, the audience can be seen as playing parts as much as the GLF were. The atmosphere itself relied on consensus for its success, a consensus which was then to be applied to the public and personal lives of the general population. In this sense, the meeting itself was political, and carried with it an agenda which attempted to enforce a homogenous morality (and normality) on to a Britain which was facing the challenge of new socio-political movements and ideas during the late 1960s and early 1970s. That participants were presenting themselves as heterosexuals was integral to the ideology, even if members were themselves secretly homosexual. Indeed the characters involved in the Festival of Light were themselves so over-blown that, in 1972, David Rudkin's short stage play *The Filth Hunt*, performed at the Almost Free Theatre in London by Ed Berman's InterAction Company (later to go on to form Gay Sweatshop), caricatured leading members of a censorship campaign and parodied the event. The play included such recognizable characters as Lady Lighthouse and Rocky Soulshine.

Operation Rupert's intervention brought private sexuality into conflict with public moralizing and identity, fracturing and disturbing the original performance with a series of vignettes and new protagonists, resulting in the nature of the performance and the space being changed. Instead of being marginalized as a group outside the Festival of Light, the Gay Liberation Front had made an immediate and visible presence inside it and the nature of the action questioned the role of other participants – if an innocent girl guide could be a lesbian, what about the mother of three who had attended numerous Christian festivals, or the pop singer whose reputation rested on his 'good-boy' image? The action therefore questioned both individual and group identities, using theatricality to displace conventional behaviour and reveal or display alternatives. The Festival of Light had been made public through intervention, not by consensus. Without Operation Rupert, it would have retained a respectable image as a public meeting which by its own agenda excluded the public. In disrupting the spectacle, the GLF showed the Festival of Light that they relied on 'perverse' sexuality and behaviour to validate their own existence through exclusion of others. The tensions made manifest theatrically were already part of the Festival's own agenda and *raison d'être*.

This early GLF demonstration in many ways set the agenda for non-violent gay demonstrations and its elements of performance and humour have been used in numerous gay demonstrations ever since. That camp and self-conscious theatricality have become the trademark of gay demonstrations is not only to do with the nature of zaps – specifically, in later demonstrations, to attract media attention and appear 'media friendly' – but also with the content, often relying on camp tradition and subversion of traditional gender and sexual identities. Operation Rupert, in particular, used traditionally repressed characters – the girl guide, the nuns, the English gentleman – to surprise and reveal non-traditional sexual identities. If the whole event had been written as a farce, its conclusion would have resulted in a return to normality, and ironically Michael James's triumphant transvestite Belle claiming to be 'saved' by the Festival can be seen as a delightfully sub-versive (even Ortonesque) rewriting of traditional farce formula. If such events have a moral – and it seems appropriate that in some way Operation Rupert should – perhaps it should be that which was identified in the conclusion to 'Rupert Bear and the other people': 'One thing was quite clear: though there might have been a time when they couldn't tell the wood from the trees, they all knew now where the jungle began'.[5]

From grey days to gay days

The Gay Liberation Front's legacy is not simply its proto-types for political 'zaps', but a wide range of gay social and cultural events that had their genesis in the early visions of 1970–73. As Aubrey Walter writes in his introduction to *Come Together*:

> Many institutions of the gay community today had their roots directly in London GLF. The Icebreakers counselling service grew out of the GLF Counter-Psychiatry Group, Gay Switchboard out of the office collective, *Gay News* from people involved in the GLF Action Group. . . .[6]

Essential to the GLF's radical manifesto was visibility, the fact that gay men and lesbians are everywhere and by coming out can dis-credit many of the myths surrounding homosexuality and challenge heterosupremacy. The GLF attempted to raise consciousness in gay people to encourage them to do this, and to provide opportunities for gay people to make their presence known. During the early 1970s, GLF contingents often made appearances on political marches and rallies, ranging from anti-Vietnam demonstrations to workers' marches, women's marches and anti-racist work. By encouraging public demonstrations of homosexuality, the GLF were flaunting British law which explicitly attempted to keep all sexual matters private and behind closed doors. Britain's tradition of attempting to deny the sexuality of its public, unless sanctioned and controlled within marriage, is still notoriously conservative and, despite over twenty years of 'liberation' and the current AIDS crisis, the agenda is still very much the same. If Britannia can bear to concede that sexuality exists, it must do so in the security of the bedroom, and preferably with the lights off. It was against this spirit of secrecy, and by extension shame, that the GLF organized events where gay sexuality could be celebrated and shared.

One of the ways in which the GLF organized this type of visibility was through a series of summer 'gay days' in public parks, also providing an opportunity to have fun and gather together as a community. In *Come Together 9*, one such event is summarized as follows:

> We come together, we share out what food we have, we play games which 'adults' are supposed to have put aside with their school uniforms: Oranges and Lemons, Throw the ball and kiss who catches it, piggyback rides, mazes . . . We kiss and talk and hold hands and embrace – women with women, men with men, men with women.[7]

The events were simple enough, but an element of performance nevertheless existed, as a ready-made 'audience' of intrigued onlookers would inevitably gather or guardedly watch what was happening. The 'gay days' would occur at commercial and public events, often in traditional family areas such as Battersea Funfair and Primrose Hill, and in less pastoral places such as Hackney. The picnics and 'gay-ins' were events which were staged to help induce and foster a spirit of pride in gay sexuality through openness in public, and it was the public nature of the act which gave them significance and purpose:

> They are a celebration of our growing love for each other and an enjoyment of our new-found freedom. At the same time they look outwards. We do our thing in the public parks. We show our gay pride to the world, and most importantly, to our gay sisters and brothers who have not yet joined us.[8]

The 'gay-ins' were also the tentative beginnings of mass demonstrations of gay pride, of the sort which had begun to be seen in America. The American demonstrations celebrated the birth of 'gay pride' at the Stonewall riots in June 1969, and marches of thousands of demonstrators were organized to mark the anniversary of the event, allowing the gay liberation movement to celebrate a time and event which became more and more significant in the face of growing hostility but also reform. The Christopher Street March in New York on 28 June 1970 became the subject of an anniversary poem by Fran Winant:

> with banners and our smiles
> we're being photographed
> by tourists police and leering men
> we fill their cameras
> with 10,000 faces
> bearing witness
> to our own existence[9]

The marches, which started in London, were considerably more modest affairs in their early stages, becoming in effect an extension of the gay days. The first demonstration of gay pride – although not the first Pride March – was held on 28 August 1971, and marched from Marble Arch to Trafalgar Square, where a small rally was held with many speakers being members of the march itself. Although small, it paved the way for the first Gay Pride March the following year, on 1 July 1972 in London. About two thousand men and women marched with banners and balloons through the centre of London, finishing with a picnic in Hyde Park. The gay-ins had developed into minor carnivals of gay love, boisterous and spirited displays of fashion and fancy which colourfully propelled homosexuality 'Out of the closets and on to the streets'. The beginnings of the most spectacular gay theatricals also marked the beginning of the end of the GLF in its original form, and internal arguments and dissensions eventually buried the group ignominiously in 1973.

By 1979, the Pride parades were attracting events at the end of the march, initially simple picnics and 'gay-in'-type celebrations. In 1983, Pride received a local authority grant to provide a range of festivities and activities throughout a week, and festivals at the end of the parade became a common feature. By the summer of 1985, initiatives were under way to involve large gay groups and to attract sponsorship from more commercial gay venues, with a large festival at Jubilee Gardens, including an appearance from the Beverley Sisters (prompting one of the attendant policemen to become frozen in disbelief, muttering only the words 'They're the Beverley Sisters!'). In one of the more theatrical stunts of that year, the cult drag queen Divine sailed up the Thames on a river boat provided by the gay club Heaven, performing his larger-than-life musical set to the gathered crowds on the river bank. From 1985 on, the end of parade festivals became more and prominent, with an open tent for the larger musical bands, a cabaret tent and a 'pub entertainments' tent and more recently funfairs and stalls. Pride is now the largest free musical festival in Europe, with larger and larger crowds moving it into bigger and bigger parks, and requiring increasing amounts of money in order to fund the event. Consequently, not only has Pride had to approach gay clubs and businesses for sponsorship but also larger and more commercial enterprises, such as Mates condoms, have now begun to take an interest in the event. And despite (a cynic might say because of) the large numbers attending ('Europride' in 1992 was estimated to attract fifty to a hundred thousand people), the events still go largely unreported in the general media and press. A notable exception was the 1993 Pride, where the serial murders of gay men in London gave a lurid interest for news items, and gave Pride its 'best' coverage ever.

London Pride is now the largest annual gay event in Britain, with the march itself taking over the centre of London every last Saturday of June (or thereabouts). It has spawned a number of local events and marches, Winter Pride, fundraisers and now has an organizing committee working throughout the year. It has been taking place for over twenty years, and many gay men and lesbians will have been on at least one Pride event, large numbers regularly travelling from all over England, Scotland and Wales in order to do so. It is a regular meeting place for many people who don't see each other at any other time of the year, and is a coming-out procession for many who otherwise lead very conventional lives. Participants may dress up or strip off, attend as part of a group, a partnership or individually, and the event is often referred to as if it was a family get-together. It has become not only a demonstration of gay pride, but also a source of it. The festival has become increasingly accessible to all sections of the gay community, now providing travel facilities, signers for the deaf and partially hearing, first-aid facilities and creches, spaces for women only and people of colour tents which aim to promote awareness and multicultural activities. It attracts lesbians and gays, heterosexuals and bisexuals, parents and children, trade unionists, sado-masochists and religious groups.

Because of its sense of tradition, occasion, and size, Pride is a kind of performance very different from any other gay theatrical event in Britain. Although it is smaller than similar gay events such as the Mardi Gras in Sydney, Australia, and the Hallowe'en Parade in Castro Street, San Francisco, Pride is nevertheless a carnival in the true theatrical sense of the term, more so even than the more famous annual Notting Hill Carnival. In his analysis of what makes theatre and performance, Richard Southern in *The Seven Ages of the Theatre* discusses the intrinsic theatricality in even the simplest 'tribal gathering':

> Provided it meets on a Particular Occasion, the elements of theatre are there – or can be called into being. We have seen that the essence of the theatre lies in communicating something to the people. So that if the gathering meets on a particular occasion, the subject of the occasion may be what is communicated to the people. And it can almost communicate itself – with the people's help.[10]

Although this might be simplistic, it points to the theatricality of the event as a public occasion, a public celebration, and this calls into being the elements of theatricality needed in order to communicate the event. Using symbolism and spectacle, it is the event itself that is communicated. What is being celebrated is gay pride in public, and those forms which communicate that are both the message and the event. That Pride should be interpreted differently by different groups signifies its intangible nature – for many gay men it might simply be a party, for trade unionists it might be a show of solidarity with the oppressed. The Stonewall riots were about both the right to party and the fight against discrimination and oppression.

It is Pride's public manner which makes it so theatrical and anarchic.

Furthermore, because of the politics around sexual identity, there is some ambiguity about whom Pride is for, and who is actually involved. If the marchers are not necessarily gay themselves, but also friends, supporters or relatives, is Pride exclusively gay? On the other hand, those who watch the Pride parade (shoppers, tourists, residents, bus drivers, etc.) might themselves be gay, but have not yet 'come out' and identify with the parade in other ways. Are they not also part of the Pride event? Or is Pride aimed at those who despise homosexuality, putting them in positions of passive spectatorship and watching a demonstration of gay visibility and strength? The elusiveness of definitive answers is a part of the event itself, which celebrates through visibility the ambiguity of sexuality – that the Pride revellers are identified as gay, or identifying with the message of gay liberation and pride, but tomorrow they might be the person in front of you on the bus, serving you sandwiches or directing traffic. The often chanted '2, 4, 6, 8, Is that policeman really straight?' symbolizes the sexual anarchy of Pride which is present and on the point of release. In the truest sense of carnival, Pride deconstructs hegemonic power and identity for its own purpose through theatrical reinvention and implosion of the ordinary and everyday. Instead of being 'other', gay sexuality becomes that which is seen, observed, possible and pervasive. Baz Kershaw, in *The Politics of Performance: Radical Theatre as Cultural Intervention*, sees carnival as fulfilling many of the prerequisites for 1960s counter-cultural ideological forms, and we can recognize many of these 'carnivalesque' concepts in Pride:

> carnival undermines the distinction between observer and participant; it takes place outside existing social and cultural institutions, occupying real space-time in streets and open spaces; it is pluralistic, able to absorb contradictory practices within a single expressive domain; it delights in the body, sexual, gustatory, scopophilic; it is accessible and it is excessive, enjoying spectacle and grotesque exaggerations of the norm.[11]

Public carnivals have often been recognized through their celebration of pleasure, and their deconstruction of hierarchical and
normative boundaries. Early religious festivals used carnivalesque
conventions to parody prevailing attitudes and structures, being
bawdy and explicit festivals of human spirit. The celebration of the
body has been visible in Pride since its early days, and may take the
presence of body adornments (tattoos, piercings, make-up, costume) or the uncovering and undressing of the body (notably
breasts, buttocks). Sex, as well as sexuality, is celebrated, often
graphically or in grotesque imitation. The carnival will often
feature parodies or imitations of political figures who have been
opposed to homosexuality (Steven Gee's 'Margaret Thatcher' has
been a regular attender at Gay Pride for several years, marching
with and often leading the very minority she attempted to disen-
franchise with Section 28 of the Local Government Act in 1988).
Dancing bands, banners and costume have now become regular
features of the event, as have such stunts as the Sisters of Perpetual
Indulgence riding pillion with gay bikers on motorbikes through
London and along the procession. Although stewarded, and often
with a heavy police presence, the parade itself is often chaotic and
casual, with participants drifting in and out to meet friends, or do
some shopping. The Pride parades give a licence to be frivolous,
confrontational, outrageous.

Yet it is this 'licence' which is problematic to Baz Kershaw,
and to myself. Is such licence in fact counterproductive, working as
an opiate against consciousness-raising and community-forming by
focusing on the freedom and liberation of a single day, at the
expense of other forms of oppositional organization?

> the specific meaning of carnival derives from its contex-
> tuality, both at the concrete level of the local community and
> at the more generalised level of socio-political history. If the
> carnivalesque is to contribute effectively to progressive
> change then it must be organisationally grounded in relation
> to wider cultural/philosophical movements.[12]

Kershaw illustrates his point by pointing to examples of British
counter-culture which he feels illustrate this, such as Greenham

Common and Rock Against Racism, to which I would certainly add Pride as exhibiting these features of oppositional culture and carnivalesque. By doing so, however, it is also necessary to look at the inherent tension of Pride's carnivalesque activity, which both gives it impetus and could also disempower it.

The danger of a parade such as Pride is that it becomes depoliticized through its form, and that such political impetus as exists in it is controlled and defused by the festival itself. If Pride provided an opportunity for lesbians to be hidden in canoes and sneaked into an all-male nude bathing ground at Parson's Pleasure in Oxford during Pride 1974 in order to disturb the closeted dons enjoying their privileged homoeroticism, then that same action could be criticized precisely for its uniqueness and remarkability, in the sense that it is a single and isolated action. Increasingly, the festival in the park has become a more and more important part of Pride, with many people turning out only for the party. This shift in focus brings its own set of problems, not least of which is funding the festival – providing stages, marquees, toilets and so on. It has been mooted that Pride should become a paying event. If this happens, it may mean that the Pride March itself disappears altogether, or becomes an increasingly marginalized event as revellers expect more for their money in the park. The Pride March, which started the festival, is also the least contained element of Pride – it's on the streets and most directly recalls the Stonewall riots of 1969. The danger of defusion of political tension is minimized by Pride's context – it is part of an ongoing struggle, and represents an event in a community's history, as well as being a focal point for communal activity and preparation the whole year round. It commemorates a movement with international connections, and is in many ways a 'gay holiday'. Gay identities do not disappear when Pride is over for the day – they become more complicated and variable, fracturing into resistant identities within the family, workplace and colleges.

Perhaps more importantly, Pride itself becomes the locus for debates about assimilation or difference. Should Pride demonstrate how normal and respectable gay men and lesbians are, thus countering the stereotypes of limp-wristed effeminates and child-abusers, or should it reveal how diverse the community is? This touches on larger questions which have never been resolved within gay communities – how different (or similar) do we want to be to the heterosexual majority? In making public sexual identities, Pride is both revealing the extent of gay visibility and making it commonplace. That such an event takes place annually emphasizes the point that it is how sexual identity is treated by society which makes it ordinary or lends it special significance. For those on the march, it provides the source of commonality, and for 'spectators' it provides a source of exotic (perhaps erotic) and fantastic spectacle. Unless it is the diversity of sexuality which is being celebrated, Pride makes no sense at all. If Pride was merely pretence and performance – that is, if alternative identities were not being celebrated and paraded – the whole event would be an elaborate sham. It is Pride's actuality, its anti-hegemonic plurality, which is its strength and challenge. And it is the public nature of its spectacle which makes it a strong and democratic theatrical manoeuvre.

The containment of anarchistic potential in a structured event is itself a deception – what is being celebrated is the survival of outlawed identity and practice *throughout the year and throughout the ages*. If gay identity existed only at Pride, it would mean nothing. To legitimize gay sexual identity – even in the simple carnivals of Pride – is to acknowledge it and therefore to give it credence. Pride demonstrates that we exist throughout the year, that the organizations carrying banners, providing floats, putting on acts or running bars are community (and more often commercial) ventures which have arisen as a result of the event being celebrated. Although largely ignored by the media, Pride is the largest and most regular theatrical manoeuvre in Britain today.

In a series of lectures at Cambridge University, later published as *The Bone Won't Break*, John McGrath finds hope for modern theatre in his reappraisal of carnival, prompted by the Russian critic Mikhail Bakhtin. It seems a pity that in discussing the enormous optimism he places on carnival as an art form for the dispossessed, McGrath did not manage to see in Pride the fulfilment of many of his ideas and wishes:

> As to the last sector of society, the dispossessed, the resistance – they are the non-people, the work-shy who have to be

kept quiet, orderly and out of the way of the Great Machine. The carnival is above all for them. To form part of an unofficial counter-culture that will enrich lives, raise spirits and prepare the way for the future, out of the language, the experience, the imagination, the needs of the people, a truly popular art . . .[13]

Notes

1.   Noël Greig and Drew Griffiths, *As Time Goes By*, produced 1977 by Gay Sweatshop, Published in *Two Gay Sweatshop Plays* (GMP, 1981), pp. 69–70.
2.   *Village Voice*, 3 July 1969, cited in John D'Emilio and Estelle B. Freedman, *Intimate Matters: A History of Sexuality in America* (New York: Harper & Row, 1988), p. 319.
3.   'Rupert Bear and the other people', in *Come Together 10* (November 1971), in *Come Together – The Years of Gay Liberation 1970–73*, ed. Aubrey Walter (GMP, 1980), p. 143.
4.   'Rupert . . . bared', from *Come Together 9* (September 1971), in *Come Together*, p. 124.
5.   'Rupert Bear and the other people', in *Come Together*, p. 145.
6.   Aubrey Walter, introduction to *Come Together*, pp. 37–8.
7.   'Gay days and GLF', in *Come Together 9*, in *Come Together*, p. 117.
8.   Aubrey Walter, from *7 Days* (6) (1–7 December 1971), p. 14, cited in Jeffrey Weeks, *Coming Out* (Quartet, 1977), p. 195.
9.   From Fran Winant, 'Christopher Street liberation day, June 28, 1970', in *The Penguin Book of Homosexual Verse*, ed. Stephen Coote (Harmondsworth: Penguin, 1983), p. 366.
10.   Richard Southern, *The Seven Ages of the Theatre* (Faber & Faber, 1962), p. 26.
11.   Baz Kershaw, *The Politics of Performance: Radical Theatre as Cultural Intervention* (Routledge, 1992), pp. 72–3.
12.   Kershaw, *The Politics of Performance*, p. 75.
13.   John McGrath, *The Bone Won't Break* (Methuen, 1990), p. 166.

Chapter nine

Queer Turf and Hetero Territory

Peter Tatchell said that OutRage was a non-violent organisation so the soldiers had to win. I thought we might have beaten one up.

The lads, sixteen of them, blew whistles at Cliff Richard for a minute – quite harmless, but it hit the whole front page of the 'Mirror' next day. This shows how perverse the society is we live in. . . .

In our film all the OutRage boys and girls are inheritors of Edward's story.

Derek Jarman, extracts from Queer Edward II[1]

IN response to a series of violent 'queer-bashings' and anti-gay murders and a series of police surveillance operations in public toilets and 'cottages', a group of lesbian and gay activists and community groups met on 10 May 1990 at the London Lesbian and Gay Centre to establish a new, direct action group which would tackle issues around homophobia and anti-gay prejudice. The group eventually called itself OutRage! and established a group purpose which summed up its aims and methods as follows:

OutRage! is a broad-based group of lesbians, gay men and bi-sexuals committed to radical, non-violent direct action and civil disobedience to:

- ASSERT the dignity and human rights of lesbians, gays and bi-sexuals;
- FIGHT homophobia, discrimination and violence against lesbians, gays and bi-sexuals;
- AFFIRM the rights of lesbians, gays and bi-sexuals to sexual freedom, choice and self-determination.[2]

The 1990s had already seen a series of physical and philosophical attacks on lesbians and gay men, and the collapse of OLGA (Organization for Lesbian and Gay Action) earlier that year had left a campaigning vacuum which the newly emerged OutRage! began to fill. A series of imaginative direct action 'zaps', in the tradition of the early GLF zaps, centred on the issues of police surveillance and queer-bashings, and lead in time to consultations with the Metropolitan Police and gay community groups to raise issues with the police and attempt to work towards closer liaison on crimes against lesbians and gay men. In addition, OutRage!'s publicization of police resources spent on entrapment and agents provocateurs at the expense of investigations of serious anti-gay crimes led to embarrassment within the police force and pressure to work with rather than against the gay community.

From the start, OutRage!'s purpose was to intervene in the public domain and raise awareness around lesbian and gay issues which were being ignored or unchallenged. Their performing space became anywhere that would make them visible to the world, and publicize their issues – often this was on the streets, in public meetings, outside (or inside) public buildings and government offices, once 'invading' the Isle of Man where homosexuality was prohibited by the island's arcane laws. Direct action meant actions designed to capture the public imagination through the manipulation (where possible) of the media. The manipulation of voyeuristic press attention reached a peak in 1991 when several members of OutRage! set up their own group, FROCS, which tipped the tabloid media off to an upcoming 'outing' campaign of prominent but closeted homosexuals. It was revealed almost a week later as a 'hoax' designed to highlight the media's own hypocrisy in claiming to denounce the tactic of outing while at the same time they were willing to be complicit in publicizing and revealing the sexual identity and practice of prominent targets. Whether this long-standing defence of FROCS's climbdown is true, or whether FROCS simply backed down from its proposed outing campaign owing to political pressure and/or the threat of legal action, is still open to debate.

OutRage! quickly developed its own 'style', drawing largely on camp and parody, with bold slogans and a series of photographic stunts which accompanied researched press releases and handouts, keeping targets focused and directly relevant to the issue of homophobia. Every action provided a 'photo opportunity', which was often a selling point to OutRage!'s growing membership. Yet underneath the frivolity, OutRage!'s theatricality has always been tailored to encourage mass participation in difficult campaigns and has raised awareness within the gay community after a period of depoliticization during the early 1980s. In particular, OutRage! have tapped in to a young and confident gay generation who are able to live openly gay lives, and who are willing to risk arrest where necessary in order to achieve their civil rights. It is this energy, combined with the experience of seasoned campaigners such as Peter Tatchell, which has made OutRage! a unique organization in Britain and has seen it outlive many similar organizations preceding or contemporaneous with it.

OutRage's larger demonstrations and 'zaps' have always emphasized their fun aspect as a tactic to draw in as many participants as possible, timing the actions in order to achieve as much press coverage as possible. Mirroring the energy and imagination of early GLF zaps, OutRage! have combined this with a hard-nosed publicity and public relations sensibility and have marketed 'gay politics' as fashionable through T-shirts, 'queer ID' cards, and safer sex packs. Slogans such as 'Queer as Fuck', and 'From Queer to Eternity' emphasized a queer culture where image, style and a sprinkling of politicization helped to develop a corporate identity attuned to a pop generation beginning to deconstruct the wholesale hype of heterosexuality as the sole arbiter of sexual taste and health. OutRage!'s style emphasized self-conscious theatricality and performance not simply as a tactic for political campaigns but also as the basis of an assertive queer lifestyle, adopting a largely American sensibility in the conservative British climate.

OutRage!'s tactics – to publicize and expose homophobia in

all its manifestations – are open to the criticism that issues are often highlighted and then dropped by the group. OutRage! is not primarily a lobbying group in the same way as the Stonewall group, founded in May 1989 to lobby for homosexual civil rights. OutRage!'s critics claim that by organizing high-profile media campaigns which often break the law, the group not only misrepresent the gay community but also attract the wrong type of publicity and harm the case for full equality with heterosexuals. OutRage! point to the tactics of black civil rights campaigns in America and the suffragette movement in Britain earlier in the twentieth century as examples for modern gay rights campaigners, claiming that 'So long as the law discriminates against lesbians and gay men, we are not prepared to obey the law'.[3]

Aware of their media influence, OutRage! have a history of returning to campaigns or conducting 'rolling campaigns' which follow through a series of protests on a similar theme to raise issues and continue public debate. By continuing to intervene in the public domain, the group discourages complicity with the marginalization of sexuality to the private – and controlled – domain of the bedroom. The assertion of gay sexual identity is a public and communal act which has repercussions in all aspects of a person's working and social life and, by extension, with their relationship with the state. OutRage! ritualize and control their political and social criticism through theatrical protest on a public stage of their own making where performance is self-consciously imitative of actual events, providing a polemical antithesis to spectatorship and passivity.

The history of OutRage! illustrates this continued intervention in public spaces presumed to be exclusively heterosexual. On 15 July 1991, with the Brighton Area Action Against Clause 28 group, they maintained a picket of the International Congress for the Family and infiltrated the stage while Princess Diana addressed the audience, using large placards to demand custody rights for lesbian mothers. The theme of the 'pretended family relationship' – a phrase coined by the 1988 Section 28 – was revisited in a more theatrical venture that Christmas in Covent Garden, where the group held an 'OutRage! Family Christmas'. Set in the busy shopping centre where traditional Christmas celebrations are held annually, OutRage!'s version involved carol-singing, the giving of presents, fun competitions and messages of support from groups such as the Albany Trust (which provides young lesbians and gays with older 'brothers and sisters'), all to celebrate the strength and diversity of lesbian and gay families. Aside from traditional speech-making, the ceremony also featured a 'Spot the bigot' competition with enlarged pictures of favourite homophobes, and the giving of presents representing aspects of equality and positive features of the extended lesbian and gay 'family'. Although the event followed a pattern similar to many Christmas services or carol-singings, it maintained a distinctly gay character, providing an irreverent focus at a time which for many gay men and lesbians can be the most stressful of the year involving the enforced or dutiful attention to biological families to the exclusion of friendship networks. If Christmas is sold as a family celebration, it is at the expense of those not included in the traditional equation, often compounding feelings of isolation and difference. The OutRage! Family Christmas not only recognized this but celebrated the diversity of what might be described as 'family' or 'community', theatrically representing tradition and ceremony in a recontextualized form. The combination of as public a space as Covent Garden, the context of Christmas, and the reappropriation of traditional forms such as carol-singing provided a coherent theatrical manoeuvre which revitalized the Christmas message of good will and cheer:

> Hark the Herald fairies shout
> Gay is good and gays are out
> Out of closets – out today
> Liberation's on its way
> Some they laughed at, some they jailed
> Some they sacked but still they failed
> To smash the pride they could not see
> Gays in solidarity
> Hark the herald fairies shout
> Gay is good and gays are out[4]

Some of OutRage!'s most controversial and spectacular actions have been designed not against the state but against the

Church and established religions. Again, this is a theme which the group has returned to on more than one occasion, intervening in internal Church debates about the role and nature of gay clergy and homosexuality in general. OutRage!'s official stance is that they do not condemn any person's beliefs or creed but deplore systematic use of homophobia in any religious philosophy. To this end, OutRage! established an early sub-group called the Whores of Babylon which took a special interest in religious homophobia. One of its first actions was an 'exorcism' of Lambeth Palace, the Archbishop of Canterbury's residence. The Demon of Homophobia was cast out in a ceremony conducted in ecclesiastical costume and featuring costumed dancers, incense and tambourines. Its use of religious paraphernalia and spiritual tone attracted a great deal of publicity, arguing that the Church's condemnation of lesbians and gay men was a form of character assassination perpetrated by the two-thousand-year-old plague of the Church by the Demon of Homophobia. The action began a series of interventions in religious affairs, including zaps on the 'Ex-gay' Christian Movement, an organization which claims to 'cure' homosexuality. OutRage! have disrupted church services and worked with organizations such as the Lesbian and Gay Christian Movement to pressurize religious organizations into adopting pro-gay policies. More recently, in 1993 an action aimed against the former Jewish Chief Rabbi, Lord Jakobovitz, after his suggestions that pinpointing 'gay genes' in unborn foetuses might lead to treatment of the problem before birth, caused controversy and accusations of anti-Semitism for both the timing of the action and its target (a London synagogue which had very little to do with Jakobovitz). What this shows is that religious actions can be extremely successful when the conventions and rituals of the religion are well understood, but can become confused, even offensive, when culturally misunderstood. OutRage! were undoubtedly right in protesting against Jakobovitz, but a more carefully targeted campaign might have spared OutRage! unwelcome accusations of cultural bias.

The ability to conduct a series of direct actions focusing on different aspects of one campaign was most successfully realized by OutRage! in its 'Equality Now' election campaign of 1992. By December 1991, it had been decided within the group to conduct a high-profile and sustained campaign to raise the issue of full equality for lesbians and gay men during the forthcoming general election campaign in order to put the debate on the agenda of all the major parties – or at least to decipher what their policies towards lesbian and gay equality were. The stated aims of the campaign were fourfold:

(a) Expose and challenge State homophobia.
(b) Pressure the government and political parties to support reform.
(c) Promote public awareness and debate about homophobic discrimination.
(d) Set our demands for equality on to the general election agenda.[5]

The campaign's main focus was 'Equality Now', and focused on individual actions centred on different aspects of state-sanctioned inequalities – discrimination within the military, and against lesbian and gay couples, job discrimination, age of consent and Section 28. The tactics of the campaign were to launch a large, media-friendly demonstration fortnightly highlighting the different demands of the campaign and to encourage debate of the different issues within the media and in public debate. The focus was to include lesbian and gay issues in the public arena as the general election approached, and to make politicians aware of lesbian and gay issues as a matter of public concern. Political space through invasion and seizure of physical space became a major tactic in the ongoing campaign as the three-month operation began on 6 February.

The campaign of disobedience that was encouraged throughout the Equality Now protests was given celebrity backing as a march on Parliament began the demand to reclaim lesbian and gay rights. Joined by film-maker Derek Jarman, Margaret Thatcher look-a-like Stephen Lind and pop singer Jimmy Somerville, hundreds of demonstrators risked arrest by marching on Parliament in defiance of the Sessional Orders which forbid demonstrations near Parliament while MPs are sitting. The staged confrontation between marchers and the forces of 'democracy' did result in many arrests, adding force to the seriousness of the march's intentions. The march's focus was given further poignancy by its meeting place – Bow Street Police Station, where in 1895 Oscar Wilde was charged with consenting homosexual offences. OutRage! used the pettiness of the Parliament's own Sessional Orders to highlight public discrimination against lesbians and gays through the legislative and democratic bodies supposedly set up to protect and affirm civil rights. The group established that Parliament not only excluded lesbians and gays from political space but defined the spaces in which democratic protest itself is allowed – and that the space for mass demonstration is excluded from Parliament itself.

The continuation of the Equality Now campaign produced more theatrical protests as it narrowed the focus of each action. On 20 February, a protest against military homophobia included the 're-decoration' of statues of prominent gay or bisexual military leaders. The statues of some of Britain's most celebrated commanders – Haig, Montgomery, Kitchener and Mountbatten – were transformed into gay icons with the use of feather boas, handbags, and other camp paraphernalia while a wreath was laid at the Ministry of Defence to commemorate the lesbian and gay victims of military witch-hunts in Britain. In 'reclaiming' prominent commanders as lesbian and gay, the protest attempted to show how lesbians and gay men were capable of serving their country in the armed forces but were discouraged by homophobic attitudes towards sexuality within the service, citing the figure that between 1987 and 1990, 306 lesbians and gay men were dismissed from the armed forces. The posthumous 'outing' campaign was again a publicization of issues affecting lesbians and gays in the military, ironically recostuming military uniform, itself being represented in the action as a costume representing and symbolic of institutionalized homophobia.

For the next target in the Equality Now campaign – laws forbidding soliciting and procuring between consensual adult homosexuals – OutRage! returned to a popular theatrical manoeuvre, the kiss-in. OutRage! had used this successfully at the statue of Eros in Piccadilly, London, in 1990 when hundreds of demonstrators flouted the law by kissing same-sex partners in public without being arrested. This action, and its continued use, proved not only that the law was unenforceable when applied to a large group of people but that the very foundation for the law was nonsensical. As well as the established kiss-in, a 'wink-in', was staged: participants acting as 'sex criminals' wearing winking masks exchanged giant calling cards with their names and telephone numbers to illustrate how gay men exchanging names or numbers can be prosecuted and imprisoned. In a further theatrical manoeuvre, groups of three gay men acted out 'frenzied bonking' in an improvised wendy-house, 'thus symbolically breaking the law which criminalises male homosexual acts when more than two men participate'.[6] Self-consciously performing and acting out illicit sexual identities and practice pointed not to the obscenity of the acts themselves but to the obscenity and absurdity of legislation which denies the right to equality even in private for gay men, and again the public flouting of laws designed to privatize sexuality and sexual identity had strong resonances for those present and for the estimated six hundred gay and bisexual men arrested for cruising and meeting each other in public every year.

In the fourth demonstration of the campaign, a staged marriage between same-sex couples took place at Westminster Registry Office, in the first-ever attempt by lesbian and gay couples to file applications for civil marriage in Britain. Costumed in wedding gowns and tuxedos, the partners were cheered on entering the Registry Office and pelted with rice and confetti to appropriate wedding music. The ceremony itself was reminiscent of OutRage!'s Queer Wedding in Trafalgar Square the previous year where couples were encouraged to plight their troth publicly. In that demonstration, public vows and demands included:

> We want the right to cherish each other and legally be each other's next of kin. . . .
> We want the right to have and to hold anywhere in the world with full immigration rights
> We want to love each other in sickness and in health with hospital visitation rights
> For richer and for poorer with partners' rights and pensions rights and insurance schemes.

For better or for worse with full adoption rights
Until death us do part with full inheritance and tenancy
   rights.[7]

Echoing the molly house marriages of two hundred years earlier,
the attempt to have lesbian and gay partnerships recognized in law
provided an opportunity to celebrate again the lesbian and gay
family, and to dress up for a queer wedding ceremony. Within the
gay community, political arguments have always raged about the
place of heterosexual-styled 'weddings', but by highlighting the
legal and civil aspects of such a union which are denied to gay
partners and placing them within the context of a more general and
sustained campaign for full lesbian and gay equality, OutRage!
staged a performance for the media which clearly identified homophobia in a readily identifiable ceremony which most of the British
public could relate to.

   The Equality Now campaign continued until 30 April with
marches and demands on the age of consent and employment
rights, and was the most visible and sustained campaign of its kind
in Britain. Yet it also followed and extended OutRage!'s tradition
of highly publicized zaps aimed to increase public awareness and
debate, raising issues within the public domain. OutRage!'s imaginative theatrical manoeuvres have become regular events in the press
and media, and have initiated campaigns such as Queers Bash Back
(organizing self-defence for lesbians and gay men), the Policing
Initiative (which meets with the Metropolitan Police to raise issues
of concern with the gay community) and in 1991 began the Lesbian
and Gay Rights Coalition which co-ordinated lesbian and gay
groups, trade unions and civil rights groups against three homophobic initiatives taking place at the beginning of the year, affecting
lesbian and gay adoption rights, sentences for soliciting and procuring, and consensual sado-masochism. Further, OutRage! has been
an important part of the mobilization of a new generation into
organizing and defending itself through non-violent civil disobedience through the use of imaginative theatrical manoeuvres.
Whether it can maintain that momentum and realize its broader
political aims is something which only time will tell, but it is true to
say that significant interventions in the public profile of lesbian and

gay issues have been secured by OutRage! in its first few years of existence.

OutRage!'s controversial, self-assured and assertive demands since 1990 have built up a legacy of creative lateral thinking which takes an obtuse angle on conventional politics and campaigning. Their theatrical cross-overs into more conventional forms of theatricality – producing a nativity play at Winter Pride in 1990, taking part in videos and the filming of Derek Jarman's *Edward II*, protesting at the *Evening Standard*'s film awards, taking part in campaigns against the BBC's inclusion of pop homophobe Shabba Ranks in television programmes – all reveal a systematic and self-conscious theatricality. Politics becomes as much about creative performance as simple sloganeering. Props, costumes and scripts have all been used to theatricalize political space and definitions. Politics creates its own characters and roles – witness Margaret Thatcher's dramatic change of appearance and conduct during her Downing Street years. To recreate space as dynamic, orchestrated, full of political possibilities is to deny the relegation of public space and public sexualities to private and restricted (contained) domains. And, although conventional political measures are not as yet in place to guarantee full equality for gay men and lesbians, systematic public intervention in the debate is an achievement which OutRage! have consistently explored and identified.

OutRage! are not unique in their approach, but their terms of reference are distinctly modern. The audience in all its campaigns is public – either in actuality or through the press. In 1993, they stole the show entirely during a meeting of the Conservative Family Campaign when they not only invaded the meeting but had infiltrated so successfully that an OutRage! member was taking the minutes of the proceedings. Overwhelming the small numbers in the meeting itself, it was OutRage! who were publicized in the following day's press and not the Conservative Family Campaign themselves. Recalling the adoption of 'conventional' identities and dress of Operation Rupert, that particular action once again emphasized how roles might be adopted and subverted. Where modern queer identities have become fetishized and made exotic, OutRage! have cashed in on selling sex sexily, aggressively promoting HomoSex in confrontational ways. Slogans such as 'Queer as

Fuck' have been systematically chosen to intervene in and against modern British (conventional and conservative) moralities, adding increasing public pressure for civil and equal rights which are then followed up by less high-profile groups, campaigns and lobbying. Far from being an embarrassment, OutRage! are perceptive catalysts and protagonists recreating public platforms for agitational propaganda and rehearsing queer alternatives to mundane hypocrisy and restraint.

Notes

1. From Derek Jarman, *Queer Edward II* (British Film Institute, 1991), pp. 126 and 146.
2. 'OutRage! Group Purpose – New Members Information'. Thanks to OutRage! for making their files available to me.
3. Peter Tatchell, quoted in an OutRage! press release for 'March on Parliament', 6 February 1992.
4. 'Hark the herald fairies shout', OutRage! Christmas Carol, OutRage! Family Christmas, December 1990.
5. OutRage! 'Equality Now!' flier, February 1992.
6. OutRage! press release, 'Gays to flout law against meeting in public', 5 March 1992.
7. OutRage! Queer Wedding vows, 19 March 1991.

Chapter ten

Raising a Little Hell

It could have been a scene from a Derek Jarman film: a slightly frail figure bedecked in gold-spangled robe and wearing a pink satin crown stood motionless against the silhouette of a nuclear power station as well-wishers shouted joyously and sang hymns.
   In fact this was reality.

The Independent, *23 September 1991*[1]

THE Sisters of Perpetual Indulgence have been performing ceremonies and rituals since the late 1970s, and have now built up not only a liturgy of their own but also a canon of blessings and routines with which to express and celebrate the variety of lesbian and gay experiences. The ceremonies they create represent events and individuals significant to the lesbian and gay community. Among the more formal recognition rites bestowed upon individuals is the prestigious canonization, where persistent and continued 'good works' for the gay community by a person (or persons) are acknowledged by sainting them. Although emphasis is placed on the humanity of their actions and the humility with which they are carried out, canonizations by their nature are infrequent and significant. Such a formal (informal?) acknowledgement of a body of work is designed to resonate within the work of others, diligently and dutifully carried out in such a spirit as to promulgate universal joy. The Sisters' celebrations and rituals, including canonizations, structure the public celebration of both public and private profiles and illustrate their close relationship. The space such ceremonies occupy is often semi-private, with an invited audience/congregation who are gathered together and referred to as 'the gathered faithful' for the specific purpose of participating in a ceremony. This may involve the use of a private space (as in house-warmings) or the exclusive commandeering of public space (Derek Jarman's canonization on the beach in Dungeness, or the late-night blessing of Hampstead Heath). Passers-by can observe but the symbolism belongs in the most meaningful sense to the participants and the gathered faithful.

The celebrations themselves represent secular gay rites which borrow from and refashion traditional liturgies, discovering contemporary meanings which can be interpreted both as spiritual (in the sense of serving a spirit of community) and self-consciously ironic, by their nature and context leaving little room for sentimentality and/or abstruse symbolism. In attempting to make such rituals not only accessible but democratic – the rituals themselves mean only what people read into them, that is they have no *inherent* power or meaning – the Sisters can be seen as combating what Dr Elizabeth Stuart notes as the traditional denial of a liturgy (literally, 'the people's work') to lesbian and gay communities:

> Depriving people of language with which to make sense of their experience is a particularly effective way of keeping them silent and disempowered. For centuries the dominant language expressed the experience of women and gay and lesbian people in terms of sin, perversion, temptation and guilt. We are only just beginning to find our own voices and language to articulate the language of friendship.[2]

Although Dr Stuart's concern is primarily how lesbian and gay Christians can reappropriate their heritage, on a more general level the lesbian and gay community has now set about creating for itself pertinent liturgies, and these efforts are strongly reflected in the work of the Sisters of Perpetual Indulgence. Her strong emphasis on community being created out of a collective rite or even an anti-historical tradition has strong connotations for lesbians and gay men where visible communities are difficult to recognize – collective activities, from drinking in gay pubs, attending gay clubs, to the collective parades of events like Pride, are the most visible manifestations of a community attempting to create for itself a sense of identity and collectivity. By their nature, events in which the Sisters officiate are unlikely to be traditionally recorded (even acknowledged) and so it seems appropriate to look at two of them in closer detail – the canonization of Derek Jarman (one of the Sisters' most publicized celebrations) and the blessing of Hampstead Heath.

The canonization of Derek Jarman

The *Independent*, in its report 'Indulgent "Sisters" make a saint of their hero', conflated reality with the imagination without ever really demarcating a boundary between the two. Imaginative space imposed itself on, and was seen as an integral part of, the canonization celebration at Dungeness in Kent, and even the potentially destructive nuclear power station in the background of Derek Jarman's house was seen not only as a backdrop to the whole event but as an unspeaking participant. In nearly all the newspaper reports in the straight press, the same inability to recognize (and/or welcome) a theatrical manoeuvre was shown – the event tended to be treated simply as a joke or as an act of sacrilege, without attention to the event's real purpose – a community acknowledging the life and works of one of its members.

The canonization of film-maker Derek Jarman as 'St Derek of Dungeness of the Order of Celluloid Knights' took place in Derek's famous garden in Dungeness on Sunday 22 September 1991. Derek Jarman's profile as an openly gay man in the film world, with such homoerotic films as *Sebastiane*, *Caravaggio* and *The Garden*, and his outspoken support for gay rights (condemning gay campaigner Ian McKellen for accepting a knighthood from the same government that introduced Section 28 and also knighted 'God's cop' James Anderton) were important elements in his canonization. Earlier in the year, the Sisters had been involved in Jarman's film version of Christopher Marlowe's *Edward II* and politely offered Derek the canonization in between takes. Although

the American and Australian Sisters had made numerous saints for
deeds ranging from providing safer sex information in bathhouses
to working for anti-discrimination legislation, Derek Jarman was
the London house's first canonization.

A crowd of invited well-wishers attended the canonization,
which was conducted in gusty winds in Derek's back garden, with
carefully laid out markers preventing the gathered faithful from
crashing into prized plants. Jarman himself recalls the event in his
memoirs, *At Your Own Risk: A Saint's Testament*:

> It's no small thing to be made a Saint, especially when you're
> alive and kicking and have to give your consent. In spite of
> the Sister's warning not to let it go to my head, I had to take
> it seriously. I am, after all, the first Kentish saint since Queer
> Thomas of Canterbury who was murdered by his boyfriend,
> Henry, in 1170.
>
> Eileen in the Light Railway Café asked 'Why are you
> being made a Saint?' 'Fate!' I answered. The local billboards
> proclaimed 'SAINT IN DUNGENESS' and now mail arrives
> addressed to 'The Saint'.[3]

The ceremony itself was the first Sisters' event to be conducted in
'High Palare' and began with 'The baying of Derek' as the proposed
saint was summoned out of his cottage home and presented to the
Sisters by the 'Best Man (or nearest available thing)'. After being
twice rejected, Derek was finally accepted by the Sisters and followed them in a procession to an 'altar' consisting of a raised plank
of wood with several 'objets d'art' placed upon it, including a large
inflatable banana and a cuddly toy. After a brief welcoming from
the Sister Celebrant, Derek was asked to explain the significance of
each object on the altar (which he'd never seen before). Espying a
urine retainer from a hospital, he explained how such an object had
proved useful during a recent hospitalization. There followed a
solemn but inspired reading from *Miss Manner's Guide to Good
Living*. In between songs of praise and good cheer (parodies ranging from 'All nuns bright and beautiful' to a version of 'In an
English country garden'), the Sister Celebrant delivered a sermon
ruminating on the similarities between life and a cup of tea, inter-

rupted intermittently as other Sisters became bored. Coming to 'the kernel, the nub, the very thrust of why we're gathered here today', the Sisters encouraged the gathered faithful to take part in a 'Laying on of hands' in order to 'take a little time to reach out and touch, to handle for a moment Dezzie's collective parts'. The Saint was then crowned with a 'bona helmet' and presented with a chain made up of plant bulbs, cock rings and pornographic pictures, and hailed three times as Derek of Dungeness of the Order of Celluloid Knights. In closing the ceremony, St Derek was asked to lead the gathered faithful 'slowly, gracefully and hopefully on the right note' in the Sisters' anthem, *Amazing Pride*:

> Amazing Pride, how sweet the sound
> That saved a nun like me.
> I once was lost but now am found
> Was afraid but now I'm free.
>
> 'Twas Pride that taught my heart to feel
> And Pride my fears relieved.
> How precious did that Pride appear
> The hour I first believed.
>
> Through many dangers, toils and snares
> We have already passed.
> 'Twas Pride that brought us safe thus far
> And all our foes outclassed.
>
> When we've been out ten thousand years
> And all our rights are won,
> We've no less days to sing Pride's praise
> Than when we'd first begun.

The ceremony was rounded off by a paddle in the sea with the Sisters and St Derek — amidst neighbours pegging out their washing and fishermen sorting out their nets and traps — and tea and cakes followed in the garden afterwards. Jarman commented to journalists afterwards that 'I'll distribute stone amulets made from Dungeness beach stone . . . I'm into the holy amulet business'.[4]

A year later, the Sisters returned to Dungeness to renew St

Derek's vows and to bless an extension to his cottage. The ceremony relived some of the moments of the original canonization, and also served as a form of house blessing. The canonization ceremonies together reflect a continuing interest in and approval of Derek Jarman's work and commitment, theatricalizing and celebrating his life and career in a confrontational style and dismantling preconceived ideals of 'role models' narrowly defined by morality and conscious notions of 'virtue' and 'innocence'. The debate about Jarman's status, as politician, film-maker and PWA (Person with AIDS) was brought into sharp relief in a series of letters printed in the *Evening Standard* a couple of weeks after his canonization in September 1991, when film critic Alexander Walker criticized Jarman's perceived role as 'the most famous living HIV positive victim'.[5] In response Jarman himself wrote:

> I find it offensive to have critics continually harping on about my mortality. It is possible to be a person living with AIDS, it is also possible to survive owing to the dedicated research of men like Anthony Pinching. This survival is what hurts the censorious most.[6]

Jarman's canonization was neither because of nor despite his HIV status, which was relevant only to the extent that he continued to express, debate and clarify the experiences and concerns of the modern lesbian and gay community. As a theatrical manoeuvre, the canonization succeeded in respecting and congratulating a man's lifelong achievements, and offered support from the community in continuing and expanding the visibility of gay artists, artistry and activism. As a performance, the canonization self-consciously created a pastiche of music, visual artistry and camp fun that imaginatively forged a 'people's work' of relevance and topicality in an environment that itself reflected the contradictions inherent in modern lifestyles. Although further canonizations are sure to follow – and are likely to reflect more fully the diversity of lesbian and gay lifestyles and communities – Derek Jarman's sainthood was an assertive, defiant gesture both in form and content that illustrated the survival and centrality of the imagination in modern gay consciousness.

In Britain, the Sisters have now carried out further canoniz-ations, largely to acknowledge people who have not achieved the celebrity status of Derek Jarman. A second Derek, Derek Cohen, was canonized as St Derek of Human Bondage because of his continued contribution to civil rights around sado-masochism and the validation of sado-masochist sexual identities. He was canon-ized in an SM club, at a time when legal proceedings against several gay men for consensual sado-masochistic activities achieved new heights of ludicrousness after appeals against stiff jail sentences were turned down. The first British woman to be canonized was septuagenarian Sharley MacClain, who has been active in feminist and lesbian gay politics for a great many decades and who (amongst other things) helped to found the Hyde Park Sapphics and Gays, a group of lesbian and gay men who meet every Sunday in order to speak about lesbian and gay politics at Speakers' Corner in Hyde Park. Her canonization took place at Speakers' Corner, and coincided with not only her seventieth birthday but also the tenth anniversary of the Hyde Park Sapphics and Gays. The ceremony managed to overshadow a fundamentalist Christian speaker who, nevertheless, was intrigued by the gathering of male nuns to his side. A posthumous blessing of homosexual playwright Christopher Marlowe, and the canonization of Tony Whitehead (most famous now for his involvement in the pioneering AIDS charity the Terrence Higgins Trust), have meant that a repertoire of unique canonization ceremonies has been built up by the Sisters in a constructive yet humorous accreditation of valuable work that other members of the gay community have achieved.

The consecration of Hampstead Heath

There they go
To and fro
The dancers in the dark.
Lovers meet
Sharing sweet
Secrets of the park[7]

Cruising in public places has been a fact of life for gay men in urban areas, particularly London, for nearly two hundred years. Deprived of sanctioned meeting places, they have sought refuge in publicly accessible areas both for the thrill of illicit anonymous sex and as a manoeuvre to affirm their own sexuality, identity and space. The closet doesn't exist only in the imagination – it affects the home, the workplace and recreation areas of British social life. The notion of 'privacy' – homosexual encounters between consensual adults taking place only behind closed doors – itself restricts the range and practices of homosexual encounters and identity. Gay sentimentalists such as Walt Whitman and Edward Carpenter have idealized the dear love of comrades, associating homoeroticism with the forces of nature, but in practice cruising grounds have proved more attractive and have become necessary in developing and maintaining even covert or closeted homosexual identities. The allure of easy contact, although it has its accompanying dangers (both from the forces of law and disorder and those who would seek to be unlawful and violent) has ensured and sanctioned cruising grounds as historical meeting places. Rictor Norton, in *Mother Clap's Molly House* has traced the rise of London molly houses alongside the 'Sodomite's Walk' of Moorfields and Lincoln's Inn. Jeffrey Weeks lists the cruising areas of Regent Street, the Haymarket, Trafalgar Square and the Strand, and both Weeks and Norton noted that theatres were often used as centres for homosexual soliciting. In *Coming Out*, Weeks analyses the importance of these areas to an emerging modern gay identity:

> In the developing homosexual underground, individuals could begin to learn the rules for picking up and watching for the law as well as the places to go. They could imbibe the rituals of social contact and behaviour, the codes for communicating, and the modes of living a double life. The subculture was thus a training-ground for learning the values of the world and a source of social support and information.[8]

The 'discovery' of public cruising grounds by moral reformers, police and the media has nearly always been accompanied by a degree of revulsion, moral hypocrisy and over-zealous prosecution that is seldom revealed during titillating revelations concerning heterosexual 'lovers' lanes'. The pursuit of pleasure in public places – for homosexuals at least – has always co-existed with the danger of violence and 'exposure' by the outside world. Our knowledge of early cruising grounds comes only partly from first-hand or confessional sources such as frank autobiographies or journals like *The Sins of the Cities of the Plain*. For the most part, scholars of gay history look to trial records for (intrinsically biased) accounts of prosecutions for homosexual encounters in public. The prurient interest in the supposedly licentious behaviour of gay men in (twilight) public places reflects a peculiarly British fascination with – and often repulsion of – unfettered sexual behaviour. It is not only in the murky past of Victorian Britain that we need to look for voyeuristic condemnation of cruising; public interest in gay cruising grounds such as Hampstead Heath has been noticeable in modern tabloids, with details printed which often not only threaten to identify individuals but also expose or reveal cruising grounds to agents outside the law who are then tacitly empowered to become 'vigilantes' in the name of moral purity. And such manoeuvres are not limited to those who see themselves as entrusted with vengeful moral codes. Actual or approved guardians are known for their heavy-handed attempts to become Peeping Toms. Spontaneous interventions by police to 'entrap' cruisers have resulted not only in tarnishing the reputation of Members of Parliament but in more direct physical danger to the individual caught in a compromising situation:

> Police behaviour towards gays often suggests a strange sense of priorities in the enforcement of the law. In South London, the few dozen gay men who turn up after dark at a hidden cruising spot among the trees on Clapham Common have been forced to flee several times nightly . . . as police cars drive among the bushes – often at dangerously high speeds. Officers questioned on the Common . . . claim variously that they are investigating an attack and that complaints have been received from the public. But one gay man who was attacked on the Common had cause to doubt their peace-

keeping role. After staggering on the road in front of a police car he was himself arrested.[9]

Hampstead Heath, the most notorious (and popular) of London's gay cruising grounds, has been the site of many theatrical manoeuvres. The Gay Liberation Front's unsuccessful attempts at preaching the gospel of gay liberation; Eric Presland's annual Heath plays, which attracted over a thousand viewers at their peak; and, more recently, OutRage!'s bonfire and Safer Sex Information/ Condom Clear-up campaign which helped to alleviate police and local residents' complaints about the 'litter' left after late-night rendezvous. The Heath's traditional image as a pleasant common for a summer afternoon's picnic has also endeared it as a favourite social space to gay men aside from its evening allure and magic as a cruising ground. It seems appropriate, therefore, that invitations were sent out to select individuals and organizations in the summer of 1992 to meet on the Heath for a 'nibble and a gulp' in order to 'acknowledge the long and seminal role that the heath has played in the lives of the London gay community'.[10]

The blessing and consecration of the Heath took place on 19 June during a brief respite from torrential rain and thunderstorms. Armed with garden flares and candles, the Sisters welcomed the gathered faithful amongst the 'flora and fauna-cation' of the Heath to the strains of 'If you go on to the Heath tonight'. With pertinent readings ('Midnite on the Heath' from the GLF's *Come Together*) and oaths to expiate stigmatic guilt, the celebration led to the scattering of seeds upon the Heath followed by an exorcism of the cruel lights of journalists and policemen. In reversing the traditional view that it is light which is welcomed and darkness feared, the Sisters acknowledged that 'We are all equal under the night', implying that the conflation of good with light and darkness with evil which is found in so many religions is not as clear as such neat dichotomies might suggest. With bells, incense and appropriately dramatic pauses, the Sisters encouraged the gathered faithful to exorcize 'that cruel searing light' while remembering the 'victims of the light', including Oscar Wilde, Magnus Hirschfeld, Pasolini, 'the spinster and the sado-masochist'.

The final ceremony, the blessing, reversed again the contradictory meanings of light and dark – 'In opening the closet door, we begin to flood the world with the light of sexual liberation'. In banishing guilt and welcoming in the spirits (and fairies) of intimacy and tactility, the Sister Benedict made plain that he was simply a man in a rather tatty habit, but that the gathered faithful 'are the people with the power to change things'. In closing the ceremony, the gathered faithful were encouraged to go forth and respect the newly created lesbian cruising ground (which later proved to be a largely unsuccessful – and certainly unpopular – experiment, partly because of fears about safety).

The blessing and consecration of Hampstead Heath was conducted largely in secret, in the heart of the cruising area, as casual cruisers joined in or slipped away. On previous occasions, as the Sisters manifested on marches, people would invariably suggest that the Order of Perpetual Indulgence should have a picnic on the Heath or bless it. The vision of a gaggle of gay male nuns in such a hallowed gay cruising area as Hampstead Heath appealed not only to the imagination but also to the Heath's exotic and fetishized reputation as a nirvana of sexual intrigue and possibilities. It is also traditionally one of the most welcoming meeting places for gay men, where no entrance fee is charged and entrance is not conditional on commercial activity, as in many of the area's bars or clubs. In his *Saint's Testament*, Derek Jarman explains that the people he meets on the Heath represent a wider spectrum of the gay community than is ordinarily found in gay clubs or bars:

> Neither of the lads I spoke to on the Heath were the sort I'd expect to find in a bar. The young Liverpudlian said: 'I can cope with the cold, I have to, I can't afford to put the heating on, so I crawl between the sheets and watch television.' His mate said: 'Well, at least you've got a television to watch. Maybe you could invite me round more often so I could watch it too.'
>
> There's an amazing amount of pretence we go through to meet people in public spaces; the drinks you have to buy, the smoke and noise. On the Heath you can be stone cold sober and meet someone; in the bars you are obliged to drink.[11]

In many ways the more traditional Bacchanalian 'rituals' of the Heath were merely formalized in the Sisters' blessing. Condemned too often by moral majorities and the gay community itself, the Heath has been 'queer turf' for longer than many of the present-day bars and clubs and has its own special allure. The consecration of the Heath was aimed not to intrude on the nocturnal activities of an ordinary summer night but to complement them unobtrusively. In many ways, it was a sideshow to the Heath's own sexual frolics and games of abandon, aiming to prove that it is possible to acknowledge the place of the Heath in contemporary gay life without voyeurism or moralizing and to welcome honestly aspects of gay identity studiously ignored by 'respectable' gay organizations and leaders.

The Sisters' Pythonesque rituals are explicitly constructed to undermine officious or meaningless celebrations so as to empower participants in the ritualization and acknowledgement of their own daily (extra)ordinary lives. Using public and private space to explore communal identities, they destabilize empty rhetoric or stale ceremonies which are often designed by religious or state institutions to exclude the perverse or different, welcoming diversity and unorthodoxy. Pragmatic in style and content, they not only incorporate traditional Christian or Anglican liturgies, but aim also at reinterpreting different religions and cultures. Thus, Sisters all over the world have celebrations based on voodoo ceremonies, Jewish ceremonies, Muslim ceremonies and pagan ceremonies, as well as those in between or aside from the major institutionalized religions. The imagery of the habit – traditionally Christian and sedate – allows for a range of public demonstrations of universal joy which are formalized in structure and dress to the point where divisions are unnecessary or analysis dissipated. American Sisters celebrate a communion involving condoms (to emphasize their protective qualities), Australian Sisters cast out devils of homophobia and British Sisters have recently introduced the spectre of Mother Mary Christmas in order to re-evaluate the Christmas traditions of good will and cheer.

Parody is only part of the rituals' appeal. If such events were only parody, they would be merely humorous (and to many people that is all they are). But the aim of such celebrations is to acknowledge – and build upon – traditions, rituals and celebrations which already exist within the gay community but are often unnoticed or unimportant. Coming out, meeting (or splitting with) partners, opening bars, anniversaries, funerals, are all part of the way we live now and develop meanings of their own. The Sisters have officiated at child namings (christenings), community centre openings and even heterosexual hen nights – all recognizing the diversity of the identities and activities which gay men are part of and which influence their lives together as a community and as part of a modern multicultural and multifaceted society.

Notes

1. Andrew Gliniecki, 'Indulgent "Sisters" make a saint of their hero', *The Independent*, Monday 23 September 1991.
2. Dr Elizabeth Stuart, introduction to *Daring to Speak Love's Name* (Hamish Hamilton, 1992), p. 10.
3. Derek Jarman, *At Your Own Risk: A Saint's Testament* (Hutchinson, 1992), p. 117.
4. 'Indulgent "Sisters" make a saint of their hero'.
5. Alexander Walker, *The Evening Standard*, 17 October 1991.
6. Derek Jarman, letter to *The Evening Standard*, 4 November 1991.
7. Eric Presland, *TeaTrolley*, unpublished script.
8. Jeffrey Weeks, *Coming Out* (Quartet Books, 1977), p. 37.
9. Brian Deer, 'Trust is a two-way street', *The New Statesman*, 27 June 1980; cited in Bruce Galloway, 'The police and the courts', in *Prejudice and Pride: Discrimination Against Gay People in Modern Britain*, ed. Bruce Galloway (Routledge & Kegan Paul, 1983), pp. 107–8.
10. Sisters' Invite to the Heath, Order of Perpetual Indulgence, 1992.
11. Jarman, *At Your Own Risk*, p. 109.

Conclusion

Never Going Straight, Always Going Forwards

The task here is not to celebrate each and every new possibility qua possibility, but to redescribe those possibilities that already exist, but which exist within cultural domains designated as culturally unintelligible and impossible.

Judith Butler, Gender Trouble[1]

Gays revel in scandal and the warping of social convention. In the guise of 'realism' homosexuals promote a society with only one standard – that of the lowest common denominator – themselves. The reason gays dress like clowns and act so silly in their demonstrations? – to show their contempt for society as a whole.

Australian Federation for the Family[2]

So dear friends, dear lovers, through this world of mine that I weave for you here, methinks sometimes I see you moving.

And I wait of you that in time you also spread worlds equally beautiful, more beautiful, for me.

[Not in written words only, but in spoken words, or the mere sound of the voice or look of the face, and in

beauties of body and limb and brain and heart, and in
beauty of deed and action, and in a thousand ways,]

Edward Carpenter, 'Lo! what a world I create', 1902[3]

THIS study of gay theatrical manoeuvres has, necessarily, been selective in its choice of material. In collating broadly defined examples of 'performance' and 'theatricality' centred on (homo)-sexual identities, its purpose has been to include rather than exclude forms and practices of self-consciously gay theatre which exist outside traditional theatre spaces, and illustrate a performative culture and recreative identity and communities. The chosen manoeuvres have in turn disguised, encoded, revealed, affirmed or asserted political, social and sexual identities in a variety of manifestations. The form of theatrical manoeuvre has often accompanied political or social sensibilities and movements – the protective camaraderie of the molly houses, the knowing innuendoes and subtext of camp, the confrontationalism of direct action and political zaps. Rather than a continuous 'history', it has revealed a series of histories, and offers the possibility of imagined and imaginative futures. The search for a 'queer aesthetic' among many quarters of activists, academics and artists is an imposition against which this study and the performances, rituals and manoeuvres it details ultimately define themselves. Sexuality and sexual identity do not, by themselves, produce a particular aesthetic or sensibility, but may focus cultural production around areas of concern or necessity: in gay theatrical manoeuvres it is not the fact that culture produces identity, or identity a culture, but that each incorporates the myth of the other. The expediencies of perversion, deviance, equality or assimilation are factors which shape, contain or unleash the imagination in an attempt to (re)create the world(s) in which we live. Social and political reality both impede and drive the imagination to challenge and/or escape notions of homogenous and homogenizing culture.

Notions of community, identity, oppression and democracy are all in conflict within the manoeuvres themselves, which invite debate around all (or none) of these issues. As manoeuvres, they are often controversial or contradictory, but it is the purpose of this book to show that they should be valued as part of a tradition or liturgy (literally, a people's work) which is recreative and in constant flux. They do not show a crisis in definitions of identity, community (or even aesthetics) but belong to an ironic and self-conscious manipulation of those ideas in asserting difference and diversity. Modern homosexualities are not timeless but of specific times and places, producing theatrical manoeuvres which represent themselves as opportunities and attempt to transcend the oppression of the mundane. Sexual identity, particularly through the reinventive process of 'coming out', is an act of choice dependent on imaginative rebellion against the closets of aesthetic, political and social structures where the means (a process of criticism and awakening) is as important as the end (the cultural product stems from conflicting desires to assert and escape from dogmatic ideologies). Where desire itself is outlawed, the law becomes the site of transgression and interpretation.

The strictures of culture, historically, have been a melting pot for (homo)sexual identities and sensibilities. The story is one of cultural democracy rather than the democratization of culture. The democratization of culture – making 'high culture' more accessible while upholding its own value and ultimately privilege – has been and is used particularly by gay men as a ticket to liberal understanding and sympathy, where aesthetic and artistic sensibilities recognize contributions by individual homosexuals, but not the community or tradition that engages in producing alternative and expedient culture(s). The debate in the arts world over Section 28 of the Local Government Act was successful in claiming that censoring images of homosexuality deprived heterosexual society of a view of itself. However, the 'promotion' of homosexuality as a valid and alternative 'lifestyle' (culture) within and beyond its own boundaries was outlawed – homosexuality became an accessory to dominant culture (partly because of its own binary relationship with it). This democratization of culture meant an assimilation into dominant culture on its own terms, anaesthetized (disempowered) by its own relationship with it. Where the campaign against Section 28 created a culture of theatrical manoeuvres, it failed to value or recognize them, resulting in a debate about homosexuality in the arts but not the role of the arts in homosexual culture and identity. The rights of the artist came before the rights of the homosexual.

The challenge of cultural democracy is empowerment, artistically, culturally and politically. The price being paid is that gay culture(s) are recognized or validated only when they enter the mainstream. The most obvious way in which the theatrical manoeuvres documented here have been disempowered is through their consumerization – camp, Polari, direct action, cross-dressing have all become powerful images without context or oppositional value. What begins as a site of resistance becomes an adjunct to the homogenous construction of identity as categorization. When Larry Kramer writes a list of 'homosexual' artists in *The Normal Heart*, his argument becomes not about a specifically homosexual culture but about the place of homosexual artists within the mainstream:

> I belong to a culture that includes Proust, Henry James, Tchaikovsky, Cole Porter, Plato, Socrates, Aristotle, Alexander the Great, Michelangelo, Leonardo da Vinci, Christopher Marlowe, Walt Whitman, Herman Melville, Tennessee Williams, Byron, E. M. Forster, Lorca, Auden, Francis Bacon, James Baldwin, Harry Stack Sullivan, John Maynard Keynes, Dag Hammarskjöld. . . . These were not invisible men.[4]

Ned Weeks's plea is for these artists to be accepted not as creators of alternative culture but as contributors to heterosexual culture. Their achievements are not invisible, but their homosexuality is. Instead of an argument about difference, Kramer concentrates on the essential similarities between these people and those who deny access to that culture and (more importantly) the mechanisms of power and control. The list is a denial of difference, most explicitly so in its exclusion of women. Does acceptance by society mean losing self-conscious identity and difference? Weeks's culture is one based on commonality – straight as well as gay men might recognize themselves in his canon of artists. The character of Weeks then goes on to plead for recognition of a culture 'that isn't just sexual' – already denying that such a culture might exist. Theatrical manoeuvres, increasingly, are concerned with the visibility of gay community and identity/identities, but this brings with it the agenda of oppositional culture which – although part of a tradition for the modern homosexual identity – is politically unacceptable for many.

Assimilation or ghettoization?

When you're very different, and people hate you for it . . . this is what you do: first you get your foot in the door by being as similar as possible; then, and only then – when your one little difference is finally accepted – can you start dragging in your other peculiarities, one by one. You hammer in the wedge narrow end first. 'Fringe' gay groups ought to have the tact to withdraw voluntarily from public appearances at gay parades, marches and rallies, but they don't seem to care whether they fatally compromise the rest of us.

Marshall Kirk and Hunter Madsen,
After the Ball: How America Will Conquer Its Fear
and Hatred of Gays in the '90s[5]

The tradition of bold and colourful use of theatricality in gay (sub)cultures has always been questioned in its efficacy for political action and expediency. With the increased demand for civil rights for lesbians and gays, complex questions about identity and the projection of identity have been raised around who or what represents the image of homosexuality and its acceptance/tolerance by society. Historically rejected as deviant and/or sick, a new movement to be assimilated within society is gathering momentum in the United States, and in Britain. The fear of 'ghettoization' and lost opportunities for equality have led to increased sensitivities around how gay culture is produced and marketed. The modern 'queer' is reflected in the growth of the London-based free magazine *Boyz*, which projects the image of perpetual adolescence – the carefree young gay man interested in clothes, fashion, music and bars, all of which happen to be located in an entrepreneurial gay culture.

Within this, the politics of groups such as OutRage! can be successfully marketed on T-shirt slogans or 'queer identity' tags, but only superficially and as fashionable accessories to a gay lifestyle. Mirroring the 'new man' of men's magazines such as *GQ*, a gay man might easily identify as 'straight acting' in lonely-hearts listings, adding the coda that 'No camps or fems' need reply. The process of assimilation therefore begins within gay culture itself which takes on the definitions, language and customs of straight society, in an attempt to adopt (uncritically) a transhistorical sexual identity based on similarities with straight counterparts. In the extreme, gay men become bedfellows with straight men on the basis of their shared masculinity and gender identities. This can be seen as the fulfilment of both sexual and political fantasies which hark back to the mythical equality of Greek sexual love between men, where what was shared was not sexual identity but male privilege and power within a highly stratified class system.

Within the call for assimilation under the banner of 'equality', those who 'ghettoize' identity and community are in turn criticized or marginalized. The American debate about tactics for equality has been simmering in Britain for many years, and is likely to sharpen in focus as the prospects of equality become realized. Theatricality and performative identities have been a target for such criticism from far-left groups (claiming that gay 'zaps' cannot be part of a larger campaign for social change), far-right groups (claiming that gays are behaving irresponsibly and 'flaunting' their homosexuality), and from within and without the gay community itself. A letter to a national gay weekly, *The Pink Paper*, illustrates anxieties around high-profile, staged events:

> No doubt Outrage is sincere in its intentions, but perhaps its members should seek to become more representative of the wider gay community before slagging them off for not joining in with their amateur dramatics.
>
> Dramatics could well be doing the rest of us trying to get on with our lives more harm than good.[6]

The tactic is to blame gays for their own oppression, dividing loyalties between members of the community and as responsible and respectable 'citizens' of society. Again, the question revolves around form and not content – theatrical manoeuvres aren't seen as having value in a social sense, but limited appeal in a radical political sense. The fear of stereotyping gay men as sensitive and artistic prevents us from seeing those cultures in which different sexual identities have been created over time, and from validating them. The 'amateur dramatics' of groups like OutRage! aren't simply a response by members of the gay community, they are part of its historic identity. The creation of community and performative identities through ritual and theatricality is part of our tradition, where no such tradition has been available. Theatrical manoeuvres serve a social function in creating identity as well as reflecting it.

In the same issue of *The Pink Paper* in which 'Rob Angeles from Surrey' attacked OutRage! for their 'amateur dramatics', correspondents also debated the politicization of the annual Pride celebrations, following a call from Peter Tatchell and OutRage! to organize the Pride March around political demands such as equality at work. What was perceived by some activists as a depoliticization of Pride was claimed by members of the Pride organizing committee as a celebration of diversity within gay communities – something which they claimed might be jeopardized by dogmas imposed on a traditional celebration of the Stonewall riots:

> The directors of the Pride trust see it as their duty to reflect, not direct and by arranging the parade, act as the catalyst for the expression of lesbian, gay and bisexual diversity. To impose a theme on the Parade such as equal rights at work would be divisive and set a very dangerous precedent.[7]

There is no doubt that the Pride Marches are increasingly representing not only community but business interests, as numbers grow and funding becomes more important in order to sustain the event. Pride's politics remain within the event itself – it is a specific cultural phenomenon in Britain, and should retain its focus within the event itself. This is not to say that it should not reflect the politics being debated within the community, and the criticisms levelled at Pride generally reflect criticisms in the community/communities themselves, about politicization, identity and the nature of the community. A perceived depoliticization of the year's most important event accompanies depoliticization of the community itself and its own commercialization. At the end of 1992, the London Lesbian and Gay Centre collapsed financially and so far no concerted attempt has been made to rekindle the desire for an equivalent. The emergence of 'Queer Street' in Soho (where a number of gay shops, pubs and clubs have mushroomed over the last two years) is testimony of the confidence of the pink pound at the expense of such enterprises as the Lesbian and Gay Centre. Equality seems to be bought on the basis of similarity rather than difference, and this is a high price to play in a modern pluralist society.

Community and identity

'Community' and 'identity' have been important, if undefined, notions in this book. In escaping definition, they have been presented as unfixed and fluctuating. The theatrical manoeuvres studied have lent themselves to pragmatic notions of identity, where gay identity is centred not on a definitive homosexual sensibility but on a range of sensibilities which are not heterosexual. In this sense, gay identity has been performative and playful, resisting attempts to be defined, controlled or limited either by political dogma or medical and legal restrictions. This playfulness of sexual identity has meant a range of possibilities or choices available outside of 'straight' definitions and which problematize strict definitions along the lines of gender and/or biological sex. Masculinity and femininity are both theatrical manoeuvres, illustrated by the 'butch clones' and drag queens, rather than remaining fixed and everlasting. Moreover, they are – as Judith Butler has suggested in *Gender Trouble* – part of each other, and are specifically problematized by gay male identity. Playing with representations of sexual identity has been an important process not in creating fixed identities but in offering a range of possible identities in any given culture. The plurality of identities within gay male culture – masters, slaves, leather queens, transvestites, transsexuals, radical fairies to name but a few – are both criticisms and reflections of male sexual identity and its performative aspects. In creating communities based around these and other identities, one method has been the formal theatricalization of those identities.

Rictor Norton notes in *Mother Clap's Molly House* that, in general, subcultures share five characteristics – exclusive social gatherings, communication networks unrecognized by mainstream society, specialized slang, a common identity with other members of the group, and a protective community of shared sympathy.[8] In all these respects, there have been subcultures and communities based on homosexual identities, and an important part in the creation of those identities has been the creation of rituals, ceremonies and communal events that help to represent and inform them. Many of these events have been theatrical in nature and content, as traditional (historical) celebrations are rarely seen, particularly in the relatively young gay liberation movement. It seems opportune, then, that such rituals and theatricality should have been created in order to promote a sense of belonging. In turn, these have affected group identity and belonging so that identity and community have been reliant on their own creation, and so that one is part of the other. Theatrical invention has been part of this recreative playfulness of group and individual identity. The liturgy – 'people's work' – of the gay community has been created out of necessity, at first self-protective but increasingly assertive. The stereotype of the artistic homosexual drama queen is a distortion of much of the tradition of homosexual subculture, a mainstream recontextualizing of necessary and supportive frameworks. The homosexual stereotype is a denial of choice and possibility with respect to sexual identity – the reality of the construction of homosexual identities and communities would suggest a broader range of playful possibilities for male sexual identities, most recently reconstructed as 'queer', where a more aggressive, political identity based on difference from heterosexuality is expressed in a multiplicity of contradictory self-definitions:

HOMOCULTURE

OUR LANGUAGE IS PERVERSION

CORRUPTION RECLAIMING ACTING

CHANGING SURVIVING SUBVERTING

EVOLVING LIFE[9]

The anti-'politically-correct' stance of groups such as Homocult – a Manchester-based group producing graphics and graffiti for street and media – illustrates the frustrating effects of staid or permanent identities and communities which provide the impetus for theatrical manoeuvres that alternately confirm and undermine traditional notions of identity, community and culture. Homocult's use of montage, reappropriation and contentious accusations/assassinations of mainstream theory, politics and ideologies confirms the tension in modern gay identities between the freedom to evolve changing representations and the search for a past, a series of histories and traditions. Ultimately Homocult deconstructs identity to the point of collapse – in 1992 women in leather fucked men with dildoes in a gay men's bar, hiding their gender identity from the men involved. 'Queer' identity became a fashionable anti-identity during the early 1990s, but is bound to collapse under its own antithetical allegiances to vacuous deconstructionism. The history of gay identities has been one of creating cultures in which to perform contradictory or alternative identities, as opposed to collapsing theatrical and imaginative spaces in self-destructive nihilism. Sponsoring a sense of playfulness in which identities can be explored is not the same as burning the playhouse down.

The emphasis then becomes placed on valuing different theatrical manoeuvres in attempting to understand the nature and culture of sexuality and sexual identities. Passion and desire have long been elements in theatre and drama, with both sexual and ideological intent. Passion and desire have also been the fundamentals for sexual identities, around which a range of expressions of those principles has been forged and manifested. If the history of modern gay identities has been the history of how same-sex desire has been presented, the history of its culture has been one of how it is represented. Both have informed each other, with gay culture at once affirming and nurturing the expression of desire. 'Gay theatrical manoeuvres' has been a useful term to examine some of the ways in which this has happened, using broad definitions of theatricality, ritual and performance. Space, semiotics and the body have been used as recognizable points of reference through which to analyse their use and changing form. The actuality of sexual identity as a performative space indicates that the binarisms of hetero/

homosexualities are false dichotomies upheld by dogmatic tra-
ditionalism, and certainly anthropological studies reveal the range
of human sexual identities and sexualities in and across different
cultures. This proves to be the basis for some optimism – cultural
restrictions on sexual identity (particularly gay identity) are a
matter of political and social construction rather than biological
necessity. Further, the continuing recreative possibilities can enrich
both our imaginations and the worlds which we inhabit. Rather
than inhabiting the realm of escapist fantasy in which we flee
persecution, those fantastic possibilities actually help to recreate,
criticize, offer opportunities for the future(s). In acknowledging and
cherishing the past, we can adopt strategies to inculcate changing,
even contradictory, identities and communities based on the prin-
ciple of their being equal but different. In this, I share the hope of
lesbian writer and poet Judy Grahn, and in closing an analysis of
gay (male) theatrical manoeuvres, it seems appropriate to look
forward in the hope that lesbian and gay identities might recognize
their own differences in order to move forwards together:

> we can see from the novels and poetry of modern, openly
> Gay writers a combining of spiritual and political strands, of
> personal and public, internal and external. And I feel a
> groundswell of hope for a renewed ceremonialism, an intact
> culture, from the increasing visibility of groups of Gay
> people from every racial and ethnic background, and the
> pouring of tremendous new (ancient) energy into tired con-
> temporary forms. We cannot live in the past, nor can we re-
> create it. Yet as we unravel the past, the future also unfolds
> before us, as though they are mirrors without which neither
> can be seen or happen.[10]

Notes

1. Judith Butler, *Gender Trouble: Feminism and the Subversion of Identity* (Routledge, 1990), pp. 148–9.
2. Australian Federation for the Family Submission to Criminal Jus-
tice Committee on the Decriminalisation of Homosexuality for the
Tasmanian State Legislature 1990, p. 13; cited in Stephen Green,

The Sexual Dead End (Broadview Books, 1992), p. 10. Green introduces his citation with the claim that if the action of groups such as OutRage! and the Sisters of Perpetual Indulgence 'was and is not satanic, then the word has lost all meaning' (p. 10). Mr Green, Chairman of the Conservative Family Campaign, spent 7 years researching his book on homosexuality and is married with four children.

3.   Edward Carpenter, 'Lo! what a world I create', in *Towards Democracy* (GMP, 1985), p. 405.

4.   Ned Weeks in Larry Kramer, *The Normal Heart* (Methuen, 1986), Act 2, scene 13, p. 41.

5.   Marshall Kirk and Hunter Madsen, cited by Tim Farrell, 'In the habit', *Bay Area Reporter*, vol. XXIII, no. 15, 15 April 1993.

6.   Rob Angeles, letter to *The Pink Paper*, 23 May 1993.

7.   Kim de Testre (Chair), Pride Trust, letter to *The Pink Paper*, 23 May 1993.

8.   Rictor Norton, introduction to *Mother Clap's Molly House* (GMP, 1992), pp. 9–10.

9.   From *Queer with Class – The First Book of Homocult* (MS ED (The Talking Lesbian) Productions, 1992).

10.   Judy Grahn, *Another Mother Tongue – Gay Words, Gay Worlds* (Boston: Beacon Press, 1984), p. 297.

Bibliography

Place of publication is London unless otherwise stated.

Alcorn, Keith, 'Queer and now', *Gay Times*, issue 164 (May 1992).

Altman, Dennis, *AIDS and the New Puritanism* (Pluto Press, 1986).

— (ed.), *Which Homosexuality?* (GMP, 1989).

Angelou, Maya, *And Still I Rise* (Virago, 1986).

Baker, Roger, and Drew Griffiths, *Mr X*, unpublished script made available by Gay Sweatshop.

Barker, Howard, *Gary the Thief/Gary Upright* (John Calder, 1987).

Bartlett, Neil, *Who Was That Man?: A Present for Mr Oscar Wilde* (Serpent's Tail, 1988).

Berman, Ed (ed.), *Homosexual Acts* (Ambiance/Almost Free Playscripts, 1975).

Blau, Herbert, *To All Appearances: Ideology and Performance* (Routledge, 1992).

Boal, Augusto, 'The Sartrouville experience', in *Theatre Papers*, no. 1 (Darlington School of Arts, Department of Theatre, 1985).

— *Theatre of the Oppressed* (Pluto Press, 1979).

Boffin, Tessa and Sunil Gupta (ed.), *Ecstatic Antibodies: Resisting the AIDS Mythology* (Rivers Oram Press, 1990).

Bray, Alan, *Homosexuality in Renaissance England* (GMP, 1982).

Bronski, Michael, *Culture Clash: The Making of Gay Sensibility* (Boston: Southend Press, 1984).

Burton, Peter, *Parallel Lives* (GMP, 1985).

Butler, Judith, *Gender Trouble: Feminism and the Subversion of Identity* (Routledge, 1990).

Carter, Erica and Simon Watney (eds), *Taking Liberties: AIDS and Cultural Politics* (Serpent's Tail, 1989).

Chambers, Colin and Mike Prior, *Playwrights' Progress: Patterns of Postwar British Drama* (Amber Lane, 1987).

Clum, John M., *Acting Gay: Male Homosexuality in Modern Drama* (Columbia University Press, 1992).

Coote, Stephen (ed.) *The Penguin Book of Homosexual Verse* (Harmondsworth: Penguin, 1983).

Core, Philip, *Camp: The Lie That Tells the Truth* (Plexus, 1984).

Crane, Paul, *Gays and the Law* (Pluto Press, 1982).

Crimp, Douglas with Adam Rolston, *AIDS Demo Graphics* (Seattle: Bay Press, 1990).

Curtin, Kaier, *We Can Always Call Them Bulgarians* (Boston: Alyson Publications, 1987).

Davenport-Hines, Richard, *Sex, Death and Punishment* (Fontana Press, 1991).

Davies, Andrew, *Other Theatres: The Development of Alternative and Experimental Theatre in Britain* (Macmillan, 1987).

Davis, Jill, *Lesbian Plays*, vol. 1 (Methuen, 1987).

— *Lesbian Plays*, vol. 2 (Methuen, 1989).

De Jongh, Nicholas, *Not in Front of the Audience: Homosexuality on Stage* (Routledge, 1992).

D'Emilio, John and Estelle B. Freedman, *Intimate Matters: A History of Sexuality in America* (New York: Harper & Row, 1988).

Dollimore, Jonathan, *Sexual Dissidence* (Oxford: Oxford University Press, 1991).

Duberman, Martin Bauml, Martha Vicinus and George Chauncey Jr (eds), *Hidden from History: Reclaiming the Gay & Lesbian Past* (New York: New American Library, 1989).

Ellmann, Richard, *Oscar Wilde* (Harmondsworth: Penguin, 1988).

Feingold, Michael (ed.), *The Way We Live Now: American Plays & the AIDS Crisis* (New York: Theatre Communications Group, 1990).

Fierstein, Harvey, *Torch Song Trilogy* (Methuen, 1984).

Fuss, Diana (ed.), *Inside/Out: Lesbian Theories, Gay Theories* (Routledge, 1991).

Galloway, Bruce, (ed.), *Prejudice and Pride: Discrimination Against Gay People in Modern Britain* (Routledge & Kegan Paul, 1983).

Garber, Marjorie, *Vested Interests: Cross-Dressing & Cultural Anxiety* (Routledge, 1992).

Gliniecki, Andrew, 'Indulgent "Sisters" make a saint of their hero', *The Independent*, Monday 23 September 1991.

Grahn, Judy, *Another Mother Tongue: Gay Words, Gay Worlds* (Boston: Beacon Press, 1984).

Greig, Noël and Drew Griffiths, *Two Gay Sweatshop Plays – As Time Goes By/The Dear Love of Comrades* (GMP, 1981).

Hall, Richard, *3 Plays for a Gay Theater* (San Francisco: Grey Fox Press, 1983).

Hammarskjöld, Dag, *Markings*, translated by W. H. Auden and Leif Sjöberg (Faber & Faber, 1966).

Hanscombe, Gillian E. and Martin Humphries (eds), *Heterosexuality* (GMP, 1987).

Helbing, Terry (ed.), *Gay Theater Alliance Directory of Gay Plays* (New York: JH Press, 1980).

Hoffman, William M. (ed.), *Gay Plays: The First Collection* (New York: Avon, 1979).

Itzin, Catherine, *Stages in the Revolution: Political Theatre in Britain Since 1968* (Methuen, 1980).

Jarman, Derek, *At Your Own Risk: A Saint's Testimony* (Hutchinson, 1992).

Jeffrey-Poulter, Stephen, *Peers, Queers and Commons: The Struggle for Gay Law Reform from 1950 to the Present* (Routledge, 1991).

Jellicoe, Anne, *Community Plays* (Methuen, 1987).

Kelley, Louise, *Anti Body* (unpublished script).

Kershaw, Baz, *The Politics of Performance: Radical Theatre as Cultural Intervention* (Routledge, 1992).

Kirk, Kris and Ed Heath, *Men in Frocks* (GMP, 1984).

Kirkman, Susannah, 'Friendly advice', *Times Educational Supplement*, 31 January 1992.

Kramer, Larry, *The Normal Heart* (Methuen, 1986).

Lahr, John, *Prick up Your Ears* (Allen Lane, 1978).

— (ed.), *The Orton Diaries* (Methuen, 1986).

Litvak, Joseph, *Caught in the Act: Theatricality in the Nineteenth-Century English Novel* (Berkeley: University of California Press, 1992).

McGrath, John, *The Bone Won't Break: On Theatre and Hope in Hard Times* (Methuen, 1990).

Mayne, Xavier, *The Intersexes* (Florence, 1910).

National AIDS Trust, *Living for Tomorrow* (1991).

Norton, Rictor, *Mother Clap's Molly House: The Gay Subculture in England 1700–1830* (GMP, 1992).

Orton, Joe, *The Complete Plays* (New York: Grove Weidenfeld, 1976).

Osment, Philip (ed.), *Gay Sweatshop: Four Plays and a Company* (Methuen, 1989).

Partridge, Eric, *Here, There and Everywhere: Essays upon Language* (Hamish Hamilton, 1950).

— *Dictionary of Slang and Unconventional English*, ed. Paul Beale (Routledge & Kegan Paul, 8th edition, 1984).

Presland, Eric, *Leather*, unpublished script made available by Eric Presland.

Presland, Eric, *TeaTrolley*, unpublished script made available by Eric Presland.

Rabey, David Ian, *Howard Barker: Politics and Desire* (Macmillan, 1989).

Rodgers, Bruce, *The Queen's Vernacular: A Gay Lexicon* (Blond & Briggs, 1972).

Seago, Edward, *Sons of Sawdust – With Paddy O'Flynn's Circus in Western Ireland* (Putnam, 1934).

Sedgwick, Eve Kosofsky, *Epistemology of the Closet* (Brighton: Harvester Wheatsheaf, 1991).

Sheldon, Caroline, *Gays and Film* (British Film Institute, 1987).

Shepherd, Simon, *Because We're Queers: The Life and Crimes of Kenneth Halliwell and Joe Orton* (GMP, 1989).

Shepherd, Simon and Mick Wallis (ed.), *Coming on Strong: Gay Politics and Culture* (Unwin Hyman, 1989).

Shewey, Don (ed.), *Outfront: Contemporary Gay & Lesbian Plays* (New York: Grove Press, 1988).

Shilts, Randy, *And the Band Played On: People and the AIDS Crisis* (Harmondsworth: Penguin Books, 1988).

Sontag, Susan, *A Susan Sontag Reader* (Harmondsworth: Penguin, 1985).

— *AIDS and Its Metaphors* (Harmondsworth: Penguin, 1990).

Southern, Richard, *The Seven Ages of the Theatre* (Faber & Faber, 1962).

Stuart, Elizabeth, *Daring to Speak Love's Name – A Gay and Lesbian Prayer Book* (Hamish Hamilton, 1992).

Walter, Aubrey, *Come Together – The Years of Gay Liberation 1970–73* (GMP, 1980).

Wandor, Michelene, *Carry on Understudies* (Routledge & Kegan Paul, 1986).

— *Look Back in Gender* (Methuen, 1987).

Watson, Oscar, 'Parlare as a second language', *Square Peg*, issue 27, 1990.

Weeks, Jeffrey, *Coming Out: Homosexual Politics in Britain* (Quartet Books, 1977).

— *Against Nature: Essays on History, Sexuality and Identity* (Rivers Oram Press, 1991).

Whitemore, Hugh, *Breaking the Code* (Amber Lane Press, 1987).

Wilde, Oscar, *The Complete Works of Oscar Wilde*, ed. Vyvyan Holland (Book Club Associates, 1980).

Wilcox, Michael, *Gay Plays*, vol. 1 (Methuen, 1984).

— *Gay Plays*, vol. 2 (Methuen, 1985).

— *Gay Plays*, vol. 3 (Methuen, 1988).

— *Gay Plays*. vol. 4 (Methuen, 1990).

Index

Index

Related titles from the Cassell Sexual Politics list:

Broadcasting It
An Encyclopaedia of Homosexuality on Film, Radio and TV in the UK 1923–1993
Keith Howes

Cassell's Queer Companion
A Dictionary of Lesbian and Gay Life and Culture
William Stewart

Daring to Dissent
Lesbian Culture from Margin to Mainstream
Liz Gibbs (ed.)

Drag
A History of Female Impersonation in the Performing Arts
Roger Baker

Male Impersonators
Men Performing Masculinity
Mark Simpson

Portraits to the Wall
Historic Lesbian Lives Unveiled
Rose Collis

The Wilde Century
Effeminacy, Oscar Wilde and the Queer Moment
Alan Sinfield